UNIVERSITY OF VIRGINIA STUDIES

THE FARY KNIGHT

UNIVERSITY OF VIRGINIA STUDIES

I. HUMANISTIC STUDIES IN HONOR OF JOHN CALVIN METCALF

II. THE FARY KNIGHT, OR OBERON THE SECOND, *a manuscript play attributed to* Thomas Randolph. *Edited by* Fredson Thayer Bowers

THE
FARY KNIGHT

OR

OBERON THE SECOND

A MANUSCRIPT PLAY ATTRIBUTED TO

THOMAS RANDOLPH

Edited by

FREDSON THAYER BOWERS

CHAPEL HILL

THE UNIVERSITY OF NORTH CAROLINA PRESS

1942

COPYRIGHT, 1942, BY
THE UNIVERSITY OF NORTH CAROLINA PRESS

To

Hyder Edward Rollins

PREFACE

THIS EDITION presents a word-for-word and line-for-line transcript of the manuscript without emendation or alteration. Necessary corrections to the text are given in the footnotes.

As with many seventeenth-century manuscripts written in a cursive hand, there was occasional difficulty in distinguishing between the minuscules and majuscules of certain letters and in deciding whether the writer had intentionally run certain words together; furthermore, in spite of the use of a strong binocular it proved difficult with a few words to distinguish the difference between the light brown and the dark brown corrective inks. Fortunately the places where personal judgment was necessary were comparatively rare, and it is hoped that the transcript is strictly accurate.

The Secretary hand of the manuscript has been reproduced in roman type; the Italian hand in italic. Decorations have been imitated in type as closely as possible. Square brackets enclose deletions; pointed brackets enclose mutilations. When the deletion is illegible, an asterisk represents an illegible letter. The only exception to this rule is the editorial addition of foliation and lineation in square brackets, and the brackets added to a few lines turned over in this edition because of the limitations of the type-page.

Interlineations are not graphically represented in the text but are indicated in the footnotes. Similarly, no attempt has been made to represent graphically deletions by pen stroke or by superimposition of another word or letter. All words or letters enclosed in square brackets were deleted by stroke of the pen. Deletion by superimposition is not shown in the text but is indicated in the footnotes. In these footnotes the word *over* means *written over* and has no reference to interlineation; thus "*c* over *k*" would mean that the writer of the manuscript had first written *k* and then altered it by superimposing *c*. Unless the color of the ink is specifically stated, it is to be assumed that alterations noted in the manuscript were made in the blackish ink used for its original composition.

The Introduction details the facts about the play which are available at present and offers the working theory that the manuscript represents

PREFACE

an augmented transcription by an unknown writer of an early lost play by Thomas Randolph. Since interpretation, as well as fact-gathering, involves the fallible human element, it is the editor's hope that the Introduction will serve chiefly to arouse the interest of Randolph scholars in this previously unrecognized play and its problems so that more facts may be assembled and a more precise criticism established.

Grateful acknowledgment is made to Dr. Joseph Q. Adams, Director of The Folger Shakespeare Library, for permission to reprint for the first time the unique manuscript and for advice on the preparation of this edition; the editor is very deeply in debt to Dr. Giles Dawson, Folger Reference Librarian, for his expert assistance in various problems of the transcription. The editor is also indebted for advice on certain problems to the late Professor George Lyman Kittredge and Professor Hyder E. Rollins of Harvard University; Professor Emeritus Thomas Marc Parrott, Professor Hoyt H. Hudson, Professor Robert R. Cawley, and Professor Maurice Kelley of Princeton University; Professor Cyrus L. Day of the University of Delaware; Professor Arthur C. Sprague of Bryn Mawr College; Professor R. Gale Noyes of Brown University; Professor Archibald A. Hill of the University of Virginia; and Dr. Walter Wilson Greg. Captain R. B. Haselden and Mr. H. C. Schulz of the Henry E. Huntington Library kindly answered questions and gave much valuable information about the manuscript of *The Drinking Academy*. Lord Monson, of Burton Hall, Lincolnshire, graciously identified Frances Monson, and Miss Kathleen Major of the Lincoln Records Office provided local information and samples of Robert Randolph's handwriting. Mr. K. S. Patton, American Consul General at Amsterdam, sent invaluable information on the burgomasters of Amsterdam. The editor is under deep obligation to the Research Committee of the University of Virginia for aid towards publishing this book. Needless to say, the editor alone is responsible for the opinions presented in the edition, and for any errors of omission or commission.

F. T. BOWERS

The University of Virginia
May, 1941

CONTENTS

Preface vii

Introduction xi

THE FARY KNIGHT
  or OBERON THE SECOND . . . 1

  The Speakers 3

  The Prologue 3

  Actus Primus 4

  Actus Secundus 11

  Actus Tertius 19

  Actus Quartus 29

  Actus Quintus 43

  Epeloge 58

Illustrative Notes 59

INTRODUCTION

INTRODUCTION

I. The Manuscript

IN THE FOLGER SHAKESPEARE LIBRARY, Washington, D. C., is preserved the unique manuscript of an anonymous play written in a seventeenth-century hand and entitled *The Fary Knight or Oberon the Second*. The writing is a cursive mixed hand of Italian and Secretary letters, with the $c, d, e, p,$ and r in the distinctive Secretary formation. Many of the stage-directions are composed in a less cursive hand which is exclusively Italian and of markedly different characteristics; but the position of some of these directions in the middle of a line of text in the mixed hand precludes any possibility that more than one writer was concerned with this manuscript. The play was written in a blackish ink, now somewhat faded, and was corrected in that ink. Later corrections were made by the same writer in a light brown ink and again in a dark brown ink.

The manuscript begins with the title and *dramatis personæ* on the recto of fol. 1 and concludes on the verso of fol. 38. The leaves are not numbered. A small irregular piece has been torn from the right-hand side of the top margin of fol. 1, mutilating the notation 2-2-0 in a later hand. The writer rigidly observed the left- and also the right-hand margin, probably by ruling his page. The concern for the right-hand margin forced him into a frequent division of his words (always without hyphens) in violation of proper syllabification. In the care taken with the somewhat mannered handwriting (the slant of which is not always preserved in the corrections), the ornamentations, and the margins, the writer was obviously striving for a neat and handsome manuscript.

The manuscript is a quarto of thirty-eight leaves made up of nineteen half-sheets sewn into six complete gatherings. The first five gatherings are composed of three half-sheets each; the sixth gathering is of four half-sheets. The page measures 6¼ by 7¾ inches. There are two watermarks. The first is a Fool's cap consisting of five long points with a figure 4 below. The head faces the left-hand side of the 4, and at the bottom of the 4 is a pyramid of three balls attached to the figure by the single topmost ball. A counter-mark of a B enclosed within a D appears in connection with this watermark. The second watermark is also a Fool's cap with the same description except that it has seven long points and no counter-mark. The watermarks occur in the following order (X repre-

INTRODUCTION

senting a portion of the five-pointed Fool's cap, x the counter-mark, and Y a portion of the seven-pointed Fool's cap): xXXXXO | OXOxXx | xYOOYO | YYYYY | OOYYOO | OYYOOYYO. It appears, therefore, that the BD counter-mark belongs with the five-pointed Fool's cap and that the volume was begun with seven half-sheets of this paper and concluded with twelve half-sheets of paper watermarked with the seven-pointed Fool's cap.[1] The average distance between the chain-lines, which run horizontally, is about fifteen-sixteenths of an inch.

The manuscript of *The Fary Knight* can be traced back to the eighteenth century. David Garrick left some of his books to his widow, Eva Maria Garrick. Various of these found their way to the London office of her solicitors, where about 1900 they were discovered in a box. On July 11, 1900, the books, along with other properties, were sold at the auction-rooms of Puttick and Simpson, with the Garrick items lots 135 to 163 in the sale. Lot 137 was described as follows:

Old Play. The Fairy Knight or Oberon the Second, Original MS. play. At the end is an epitaph on the "Virtuous lady Frances Monson, deceased April 16th, an. '58"; also some verse and prose of a devotional character, calf. sm. 4to. Saec XVII.

This volume was purchased by the London bookseller Pearson, who sold *The Fary Knight*, minus the calf binding, the epitaph, and the devotional verse and prose, to Mr. Folger. Efforts to trace the appended manuscript material have been unsuccessful.

The seven-pointed Fool's cap paper, the size of the page, and the handwriting of *The Fary Knight* are the same as those of the anonymous manuscript play *The Drinking Academy*, now preserved in the Henry E. Huntington Library and Art Gallery, San Marino, California. *The Drinking Academy* is made up of gatherings of three half-sheets with a final gathering of four half-sheets. The fact that in each play the writer was able, before beginning the final gathering, to estimate the need for an extra half-sheet is a partial indication that he was transcribing another manuscript, but it does not necessarily indicate that originally the two plays were written and bound separately. Under ordinary circumstances scribes and printers of collections or of works with strongly marked sec-

---

[1] W. A. Churchill, *Watermarks in paper . . . in the XVII and XVIII centuries . . .* (Amsterdam, 1935) lists a five-pointed Fool's cap with the 4, the balls, and the counter-mark of B within D as no. 356 (Plate CCLXXI), found among English parliamentary papers dated 1660. The two Fool's caps are not quite the same, but the first seven half-sheets of *The Fary Knight* are probably a variant of the same paper. The seven-pointed Fool's cap without counter-mark cannot be identified in any work on watermarks published to date.

INTRODUCTION

tions endeavored to begin each work or section with a fresh gathering so that the volume might be readily broken up if necessary. That the same three inks found in *The Fary Knight* are also present in *The Drinking Academy*, together with the identical paper, shows that the two plays were transcribed within the briefest interval, and the presumption follows that they were bound together by the writer in the same volume. The cuts in the backs for the binding cords match precisely in both, and both have the edges gilt. The rounding of the back of *The Fary Knight* indicates that it began the volume and composed approximately one-half or more of the total. The manuscript of *The Drinking Academy* unfortunately has become so detached that the curve of its back cannot be determined. The seven points and the lack of a counter-mark in the paper of the *Academy* seem to link it with the final gatherings of *The Fary Knight* rather than with the five-pointed, counter-marked paper of the initial gatherings. It is a not unreasonable conjecture that the *Academy* probably followed *The Fary Knight* in the Garrick volume and that the auction cataloguer, failing to observe the separate title page, catalogued the two manuscripts as one play, according to the initial title-page. Considerable support is lent to this conjecture by the fact that Pearson sold *The Drinking Academy* to Mr. White in February, 1901, within seven months of the sale of the Folger manuscript.[2]

II. The Date of the Manuscript

There are two definite pieces of evidence which fix the limits for the date of the composition of the present manuscript. *The Fary Knight* in its present form borrows extensively from Ben Jonson's *Alchemist* and *Masque of Queens*, and from James Shirley's *Traitor* and *Young Admiral*. The latest play which the editor has discovered laid under contribution is *The Young Admiral*, licensed for acting on July 3, 1633, and printed in 1637. The nature of the verbal borrowings indicates almost certainly that the writer had the printed copy of Shirley's play before him as he wrote. The close similarity of the counter-marked five-pointed Fool's cap watermark in the paper of *The Fary Knight* to a mark found in parliamentary papers of 1660 is without value as precise evidence, although it might not be too dangerous a conjecture, with

---

[2] The links between the two manuscripts are treated in detail in F. T. Bowers, "Problems in Thomas Randolph's *Drinking Academy* and its Manuscript," *The Huntington Library Quarterly*, I (1938), 193-96.

INTRODUCTION

this particular watermark, that not more than a decade separated the two papers.[3] The lack of Commonwealth allusions in *The Fary Knight* is purely negative evidence.[4] If the reference to a burgomaster of Amsterdam in lines 60-63 is not to Dirck Bas in 1621-23 (which seems almost certain) but instead to Dr. Gerard Schaep who arrived in England on December 15, 1651, and left on June 30, 1652, the date of the manuscript could be set as approximately 1651-52, but the identification of Schaep with the allusion is very questionable.[5] The epitaph on the death of Frances Monson on April 16, 1658,[6] which was bound in with *The Fary Knight* in the volume in Garrick's possession, provides the safest, although a not entirely positive upper limit.[7] The most reasonable date for the writing of the manuscript would be sometime between the years 1637 and 1658, with a rather decided preference for 1657-58.[8] The transcriber is at present unknown.

III. The Transcriber of the Manuscript and His Methods

The writer of this manuscript has been called a transcriber because an examination of the corrections in *The Fary Knight* shows that he was copying from another manuscript and, moreover, one not his own. Various of these alterations are simple corrections of errors caused by haste in copying, but of considerable importance is the fact that the writer seems to have made certain changes in the system of spelling between the original manuscript and the present copy, noticeably the change of final *i* or *ie* to *y*. Some of these he caught at the very moment

---

[3] For the Fool's cap watermark and its general dating, see Edward Heawood, "Papers Used in England after 1600," *The Library*, XI (1930), 279-80.

[4] The suggestion that "*The Prodigall Scholar*, a Comedy by Tho: Randall," entered at Stationers' Hall on June 29, 1660, may possibly be *The Drinking Academy* is apt but purely conjectural since the play was not published.

[5] See pp. xxxi-xxxiii, below.

[6] The Frances Monson of the epitaph was the wife of Anthony Monson of Northorpe, Lincolnshire. She died on April 16, 1658, and was buried in the churchyard of St. Pancras Church, London.

[7] If, as the available evidence suggests, *The Drinking Academy* succeeded *The Fary Knight* in the Garrick volume, the epitaph and the devotional verse and prose would have followed the *Academy* instead of *The Fary Knight* as stated in the Puttick and Simpson catalogue. But the final gatherings of both plays are complete, and the wording of the cataloguer (which rather ambiguously implies that the epitaph and other matter was a part of the same manuscript) is the only evidence at present available to link the epitaph with the transcriber of the plays until the missing material is found and identified as written by the same hand on the same paper. Since the two plays seem to have been written, and probably bound together, within a very short space of time, it is most likely that a third small manuscript by the writer of the plays was also included. The fact that *The Fary Knight* has six gatherings and the *Academy* three and that the Folger manuscript appears to have composed about a half of the whole volume, suggests either two or three more gatherings, or about twelve to eighteen or twenty leaves now lost.

[8] For possible evidence confirming the late date, see below, p. xlii, n. 36.

Witch:1 Well done my fiue for this thou then shalt sucke
         My bloud untill my graines be quiet dried vp.

                    Enter the 2 Witch

         Speake hag where hast thou bin?
         What hast thou done what dost thou bring?

Witch 2 I haue bin gathering Cypruss bowes
         Nightsheade and poppy that growes
         In yonder church yard where I haue
         Kill'd a sexton making a graue

                    Enter the 3 Witch

Witch 1 Whereare you? If I charge you tell
         Why I did delay my spell?

Witch 3 I heard you maime and I went to call
         The snake breed vnder yonder wall.
         I spoake a spell and out they came
         And heere is their blou with toadstones.

Witch 1 Well done my hag for this thou then shalt be
         In our great art the next to me.

                    Enters a 4 Witch

         An obdurlate what cause this delay
         Thou sluggish hag, I charge thee straight to say

Witch 4 I haue bin gathering wolues haires
         The mad dogs fome and adders eares
         A mandrake out of the earth I haue torne
         Heere is all this what wold you haue more.

INTRODUCTION

of writing. Thus in line 29, *enemy*, the writer made the *i*, dotted it, and then apparently before going on to the next word changed the *i* to *y*. Other examples of this change in spelling occur in *my* (l. 139) and in *Why* (l. 148). Equally indicative of copying is the omission of necessary words. The best example comes in lines 1312-15. Craft is delaying Losserello's pursuit of the supposed giant by urging him first to procure a magic sword. The Folger manuscript had originally:

> Craf: But arm'd sir with this inchanted steele you might me
> ete Mars in the feeld and make him crey quarter.
> Craf: No I can not my granam hath sent me of an errant.

It seems incredible that a composing author would omit between the two the necessary speech of Losserello's on which Craft's second speech depends for its meaning. Yet it is a common error in copying. Apparently the transcriber realized his error almost immediately, for with what may be the same pen for part of the line, he squeezed in between Craft's two speeches:

> Los: Well Ile go fech it? wilt thou go with me?

Other omissions indicative of hasty copying are shown by the interlining of *so* in line 45, *cow* in line 87, *O ye celestiall powers* in line 245, *be* in line 1136. Further evidence is furnished by line 299, among others, where Oliver's speech is first written as a part of Covet's before being deleted. Such an occurrence seems to indicate that a change in speaker was not marked by a separate line in the manuscript copied from, and that the writer swept on without noticing the abbreviation for Oliver separating the start of his speech in the same line as the conclusion of Craft's. Again, in lines 409-63 the proper speaker has been mistaken and then corrected, since in a number of speech headings *Craft* has been written over the incorrect *Couet*. Such an error, almost impossible for a composing author, could be explained as the act of a transcriber confused by speeches perhaps headed in the original manuscript only by the letter *C*.[9] An uncorrected error is found in the stage-direction in lines 831-32, which reads *Exeunt veneficæ Omnes præter jam*. This makes no sense, but if we read *ūam* (i.e., *unam*) for *jam*, the correct meaning is given, since one witch does indeed remain behind on the stage. And *ūam* could be misread *iam* by a transcriber.

---

[9] These errors were not caused by adding the speech headings later, since the same pen seems to have written both heading and speech in each case. This is of importance because one pen became worn out and a new pen was substituted in the middle of this passage.

INTRODUCTION

The changes listed above are relatively simple and are concerned largely with correcting errors made in the transcribing. There is, however, another form of alteration in the manuscript which gives us glimpses of what seems to have been some occasional amplification in the individual speeches from the original. For instance, in ll. 579 ff. the original manuscript had probably borrowed direct from *The Alchemist*, and Craft is repeating Jonson, "Better language she approches downe one your knees and wrig"; at this point, however, the transcriber seems to have stopped copying *wriggle* from the manuscript, deleted the incomplete *wrig*, and substituted "anske her blessing," *et cetera*. A question by Losserello intervenes before the writer returned to Craft, who answers the question and only then proceeds with his speech, "He will come by and by he is with in a drinking, now downe one y^r knees and wriggle she hath a stately presence." Another prominent example occurs in ll. 197-218. Politico asks Craft where he comes from, and Craft replies, "ffrō the blest Elizium happy fary-land." The writer then began Politico's answer from what was probably the text of his manuscript, "ffrō fairy. o doth" not the mighty Oberon rule there? But after copying *o doth* he changed his mind, deleted the two words, and substituted *land?* This change gave the opportunity for what seems to be an augmentation describing fairyland (including a borrowed phrase from Shirley) until the original manuscript version is returned to in l. 218, "Doth not the mighty Oberon rule ther?" Another example occurs in ll. 1532 ff. Shift is encouraging Covet to hang himself, and says, "I am content to be your executioner." At this point the writer deleted *be your executioner* before proceeding with the expansion, "pleasure so much your naibors as to be y^r executioner." Such minor examples as the following are common: in l. 845 the writer started "carry my sword be"; he then deleted *be* and added "and sheld" before resuming with "before me."

The transcriber of this manuscript at work on an augmentation can be traced in such a passage as ll. 712 ff., borrowed largely from Ben Jonson's *Masque of Queens*. The Witch begins a line, "Nor yet." Immediately the writer decides expansion is called for, and forgetting to delete *Nor yet* he begins a new line with a couplet borrowed very closely from another part of *The Masque of Queens*. He alters the precise wording of this couplet just enough, however, so that when he comes to the second line he is forced into Jonson's rhyme of *stars* for *wars* one foot too soon. Since the couplet is impossible, he deletes it

INTRODUCTION

and tries another which is a freer paraphrase employing different rhymes. This couplet is followed by its successor in Jonson taken over almost verbatim. A three-word charm intervenes, and only then does the writer return where he had left off and, copying either direct from Jonson or from the original manuscript which had been influenced by Jonson, begins the line, "Nor yet my rage begins to swell."

To summarize, four stages of correction and alteration are exhibited in the manuscript. In the first stage come corrections and alterations made at the time of writing before the next word was set on paper: changes in spelling, as *enemi* to *enemy* (l. 29), of *drauft* to *draught?* (l. 542); deletion of errors, as *farg* and substitution of *fary* (l. 974), or of *that* and substitution of *thanke* (l. 137); expansion of the text as in the addition of *and sheld* after *sword* (l. 845) and the various examples given above; deletion of unsatisfactory words and the substitution of more desirable ones, as in *fortunat* for *happy* (l. 219), or the substitution (ll. 713-714) of a paraphrase for a direct borrowing from Jonson.

In the second stage come corrections also in the blackish ink used for the text but made presumably after the entire play was copied, although in some cases the time of correction cannot be determined: changes in spelling, as the addition of *t* to *confiden* after the following word had been written (l. 523); addition by interlining of words necessary to the meaning, as in the interlining of *O ye celestiall powers* (l. 245); addition by interlining of words to expand or improve the meaning, as in the interlining of *the red sea boast* (l. 178); deletion of unsatisfactory words and interlining of more desirable ones, as in *howers* for *days* (l. 510); substitution by writing over another word, as in *labored* written over *elaborat* (l. 3), or *Losso* over *Craf* (l. 636).

In the third stage come corrections and alterations made in a light brown ink, followed by the fourth stage of corrections and alterations made in a dark brown ink. Both inks run through the whole manuscript, and their order can be proved by the changes that took place in *surely victorious* (l. 146) in which alterations made in the light brown ink were subsequently deleted and further corrections made in the dark brown ink. There is no difference in the type of corrections made in these two inks. The writer was looking over the manuscript chiefly for the mending of errors and less for opportunities to improve the text. The classes of changes made in these two inks are: correction of outright errors, as *his* written over *their* (The Speakers, l. 10) or *Craft* over *Couet* (l. 413); the interlining of omitted words necessary for the sense,

INTRODUCTION

as in the interlining of *is* (l. 24); the mending of faulty spelling, as in *valior* (l. 89), the addition of *t* to *heigh* (l. 95), and the change of *m* to *M* in *Mars* (l. 94); the addition of punctuation, as the insertion of an exclamation mark after *stars* (l. 94) or of a full stop after *y°* (l. 418); the addition of stage-directions, as in lines 114-16; and finally a few corrections for improvement in diction, as the interlining of *worme* over deleted *animal* (l. 212) or the addition of the last two ciphers in 1000000 (l. 1429).

The Drinking Academy, the companion manuscript to *The Fary Knight*, was attributed some years ago to Thomas Randolph.[10] Correspondingly, a conjectural case can be made for the original authorship of *The Fary Knight* by Thomas Randolph as a play written about 1623-24 for Westminster School. Since the Folger manuscript is definitely not in Thomas Randolph's handwriting, and since the borrowings from Shirley's *Young Admiral* were probably made at least two years after Randolph's death, *The Fary Knight* in its present form would then represent an augmented transcription of an earlier Randolph work, made about 1657-58 by some unknown writer like the F. J. who in 1651 published an expanded version of Randolph's *Hey for Honesty*. An examination of the sources, borrowings, and probable original date will clarify the ascription to Randolph of the play on which the present manuscript is based.

IV. Sources and Analogues

The plot of *The Fary Knight*, which concerns the cheating of various gulls by the promise that they will inherit the kingdom of fairyland, was drawn from no single source. A good example of the cheat in its simplest form is found in 1595. One Judith Philips asserted that she could multiply gold by the aid of the fairies, and procured money from a victim as well as the gift of a capon and turkey to be sent as an offering to the King of the Fairies.[11] It was only one step farther to

---

[10] For this attribution and the consequent discussion, see Cyrus L. Day, "Thomas Randolph and *The Drinking Academy*," *Publications of the Modern Language Association of America*, XLIII (1928), 800-09; G. C. Moore Smith, "*The Drinking Academy* and its Attribution to Thomas Randolph," *PMLA*, XLIV (1929), 631-33; *The London Times Literary Supplement* (Sept. 4, 1930), and *The Review of English Studies*, VI (1930), 476-83; H. E. Rollins and S. A. Tannenbaum, *The Drinking Academy* (Cambridge, Mass., 1930), pp. x-xiii; H. E. Rollins, "Thomas Randolph, Robert Baron, and *The Drinking Academy*," *PMLA*, XLVI (1931), 786-801; F. T. Bowers, "Problems in Thomas Randolph's *Drinking Academy* and its Manuscript," *The Huntington Library Quarterly*, I (1938), 189-98, and "Ben Jonson, Thomas Randolph, and *The Drinking Academy*," *Notes & Queries*, CLXXIII (1937), 166-68.

[11] This cheat is alluded to in *A Quest of Enquirie, by women to know, Whether the Tripe-*

INTRODUCTION

the disguising of accomplices as fairies in order to gain more credence from the gull. Thus we read in 1613 that John West and his wife secured considerable sums from a gull under the pretext that they would multiply his gold with fairy aid. When the gull grew restive at the delay in accomplishment, the Wests brought him to a place where their servants dressed as fairies and elves were sitting on moneybags labeled with his name.[12]

The use of a fairy or devil disguise for the perfection of a cheat was a fairly common device on the Elizabethan stage. In the Paul's play *The Bugbears* (*c.* 1565), possibly by John Jeffers, rogues secure money by haunting a house in the disguise of demons (IV. ii). Falstaff is tricked by disguised fairies and elves in Shakespeare's *Merry Wives of Windsor* (V. v) of 1600-01. In the anonymous *Puritan* (1606) two rogues disguise themselves as a conjurer and the devil in order to perfect a cheat. In Fletcher's *Nightwalker* (1614, revised 1633) a gentleman cozened of his lands deceives the usurer into returning them by a show of Furies and an Angel (IV. i). A fairy disguise helps to enrich the rogues of the anonymous *Honest Lawyer* (sigs. G2^v-G3) of 1616. Children disguised as supernatural beings aid a mock conjuring trick (V. iii) in Fletcher's *Chances* (1615, revised 1625); in Fletcher's *Fair Maid of the Inn* (lic. 1626) children disguised as spirits aid a gulling trick (IV. ii). In Shirley's *Maid's Revenge* (1626) a disguised accomplice aids a mock conjurer (III. ii); in his *Constant Maid* (1637-38) a usurer is gulled by rogues in disguise (III. ii). In Peter Hausted's *Rival Friends* (1632) a rogue disguised as Oberon gulls Stipes in the belief that he is being transformed into a gentleman (sigs. L2-L4).

The search for a mortal heir to fairyland which motivates the cheat in *The Fary Knight* was probably suggested by the old romance *Huon of Bordeaux* (mentioned in line 156), but the author drew directly on Ben Jonson's *Alchemist* (1613) for the foundation of the gulling. In *The Alchemist* Dapper is introduced to Dol Common disguised as the Fairy Queen, and after humorous difficulties with her fairy attendants procures a lucky gambling charm and the negligent promise of some thousands of acres in fairyland. Various details of the enchanting of

---

wife was trimmed by Doll yea or no. Gathered by Oliver Oat-meale [1595], reprinted in "Elizabethan England in Gentle and Simple Life," *Occasional Issues of Unique or Very Rare Books*, ed. A. B. Grosart, XIV (1881), 153, 156.

[12] *The severall notorious and lewd Cosenages of John West and Alice West, falsely called the King and Queene of Fayries* [1613], reprinted in W. C. Hazlitt, *Fairy Tales, Legends and Romances Illustrating Shakespeare* (London, 1875).

INTRODUCTION

Losserello and Politico are obviously imitated from Jonson's play, and there are various verbal borrowings. In the scene where disguised witches brew an infernal potion as part of the trick on Losserello, Jonson's *Masque of Queens* (1609) has been heavily laid under contribution. Item after item of the magic ointment is lifted word for word or in paraphrase from Jonson, and on occasion whole lines of verse are taken over bodily. The incantation in Shakespeare's *Macbeth* (1605-06) seems to have exerted no direct influence, but there may be a few doubtful indications that the writer possibly had seen Middleton's *Witch* (1609?). Some details are drawn from Ovid's *Metamorphoses*, Lucan's *Pharsalia*, and the fifth *Epode* of Horace. Extracts from these three works had been given in Jonson's notes to *The Masque of Queens*, but the writer went direct to these sources for some details not cited by Jonson. A few possible reminiscences of Seneca are found. Finally, extensive borrowings in conception and language are made from Shirley's *Young Admiral* (lic. July 3, 1633, and printed in 1637) to form a large part of the comic incantation scene. Shirley's *Traitor* (1631) is laid under heavy verbal contribution in the combat between Politico and Losserello, and in the trial of Politico.

With the exception of the numerous parallels to Thomas Randolph's known plays, the writer's other borrowings were slight. The crowning of Falstaff with antlers in *The Merry Wives of Windsor* probably suggested the specific decoration of Losserello in the final scene, but the suggestion for some such humorous device had been forecast by the mock crowning of Politico with an otacousticon, a detail borrowed from Tomkis's *Albumazar* (1615). There are a few verbal borrowings from Philip Sidney's *Lady of May* (1578) and resemblances to Peter Hausted's *Rival Friends* (1632). The hanging-ballad in Fletcher's *Bloody Brother* (1616-22) may have suggested Politico's effusion in *The Fary Knight*. In order to aid the political satire on Spain which crops up in the play, the scene is apparently laid in Spain, and as in Dekker's *Whore of Babylon* (1607) England is conceived as fairyland. Various of the characters' names are taken from Jonson, and the writer is under his general influence in matters of language. There are also some reminiscences of Beaumont and Fletcher.

V. Authorship

Although the manuscript of *The Fary Knight* is definitely not a Randolph holograph, the play, like *The Drinking Academy*, seems to

INTRODUCTION

have a definite connection with Thomas Randolph. The raising of Lady Pecunia's ghost, together with Alecto and a Pluto-Plutus, as part of a confidence game in *The Drinking Academy* finds a close counterpart in the tricking of Losserello, Politico, and Covet by pretended witches and fairies in *The Fary Knight*. In both plays the rogues preparing to disguise themselves quarrel over priority in dressing and are forcibly separated by their leader. In both the early arrival of the gulls causes them to flee in haste. Jocastus, the gulled shepherd of Randolph's *Amyntas*, believes himself, like Losserello, a fairy knight and is cheated by a rogue pretending to be Oberon. Like Losserello and his order of the cornucopia, Jocastus is decorated with the order of the tingle-tangle. Both Dorylus and Craft exchange acres in fairyland for the more substantial holdings of their gulls. As Losserello insists that Craft be enchanted with him, so Jocastus tries to persuade his servant Bromius to take moly to share in his transformation. In each play the dupe is disillusioned by the abrupt doffing of the cheater's disguise as Oberon:

> On thy head I put my crowne,
> On thy backe my purple gowne,
> Whilst my selfe I do become
> Honest Craft not Oberone. ha ha ha! [*F. K.*, ll. 1869-72]

> In chairs of pearl thou plac'd shalt be,
> And empresses shall envy thee,
> When they behold upon our throne
> Jocasta with her ——— Dorylas.
>   Ha, ha, ha! [*Amyntas* (ed. Hazlitt), I, 366].

Losserello cries, "Am I thus guld cheatd?" and Jocastus, "Am I deceiv'd and cheated, gull'd and fool'd?" In *The Jealous Lovers* (III. vii) Asotus for his own amusement pretends to be Oberon.

The mock drinking scene of *The Fary Knight* in which Spendall's soldiers toss off their pots at the military command "give fire," is close in conception to the initiation ceremonies of the scholars in *Aristippus* (itself reminiscent of *The Tempest*) with the drinking at the command, "Kiss the book." Spendall's address to his army in the same scene is very like the address of Penia-Poverty to her soldiers in *Hey for Honesty* (III. i), as is the ignominious rout of both armies. Like Chaunus in *The Muses' Looking Glass* (III. ii) Politico boasts of the foreign countries which have begged him to become their ruler. The trial of Politico in *The Fary Knight*, although based on an incident in

INTRODUCTION

Shirley's *Traitor*, is close to the sexton's mock trial of himself in *The Jealous Lovers* (IV. iv) which shows a verbal resemblance to another scene in *The Fary Knight* (ll. 919 ff.). Craft in *The Fary Knight*, Timothy Shirk in *The Drinking Academy*, and the Pedlar in *The Conceited Pedlar* introduce themselves to the audience and explain their business by acknowledging the audience's curiosity about their "profession." Spendall is the name of the prodigal in *The Fary Knight*, and in *Hey for Honesty* (II. iv) Penia-Poverty is called the eldest daughter of Asotus-Spendall. Asotus is the name given to the prodigal in *The Drinking Academy*.

The characteristic oaths and asseverations, the observance of the unities with especial attention to the unity of time—all found in *The Drinking Academy*—are preserved in *The Fary Knight*. The deification of sack and the love of drinking so prominent in Randolph's other works find similar expression at length. The typical mannerisms of character portrayal persist, especially the exuberant glee of such characters as Losserello and Simplicius catching up an idea on its introduction and gloating over it.

Any actual connection of Randolph with *The Fary Knight*, however, must rest not only on evidence for a date within the years of his dramatic activity but also on the appearance of the characteristic style of his named plays, of which only a brief survey can be permitted here since parallels are cited in detail in the notes. These parallels fall roughly into three classes. The first is the outright borrowing or close paraphrase in language when borrowed situations are treated. As Spendall before consenting to enter fairyland inquires, "Is ther the life of man ther? is ther sacke?" (l. 1817), so in *Amyntas* (I, 308) the foolish Mopsus on being promised a place in fairyland asks whether his particular love is to be found, "But is there any Ladybirds there?" Oberon, fairyland, and Utopia are linked in *The Fary Knight* and *Amyntas*. Craft styles himself "lord of the Antipodes and great Eutopia" (l. 1556), while in *Amyntas* one reads,

> out-talk the bravest parrot
> In Oberon's Utopia. [I, 279]

Craft, as Oberon, is addressed as "my stately king of pigmies" (l. 1561) in allusion to his youthful fairy attendants. In *Amyntas* (I, 325) Dorylas disguised as Oberon demands:

> Walk not I
> Like the young Prince of Pigmies?

INTRODUCTION

In both plays the rogues satirically comfort the gulls for the loss of their earthly revenues by reminding them that they have "fairyland enough."

The prologue to *The Fary Knight* begins,

> Not in heigh numbers we intend to bring
> The fates of Princes in a labored scene.

Similarly, the heights are disclaimed in the prologue to *Amyntas*,

> Gentlemen, look not from us rural swains
> For polish'd speech, high lines, or courtly strains,

and in "To the Reader" of *The Jealous Lovers*,

> I confess no heights here, no strong conceits.

There are numerous verbal parallels between *The Fary Knight* and *The Drinking Academy*, some of which coincide with the scene in both where the rogues disguise themselves before the cheat:

Giue me the viserd. ffaith thou needest none, thy face is like a visard. [*F. K.*, ll. 362-63]

Your face wold scare any body. it is a pretty natural visard you haue on. [*D. A.*, ll. 661-62]

Whist, some body comes. runne or we are betraide. [*F. K.*, l. 387]

here is Knowlittle and his tribe all ready. lets in or we are betray'd. [*D. A.*, ll. 706-07]

In both plays the disguised rogues secure the keys to the gulls' treasure and send underlings off to fetch it.

Pollitico send for the monies presently this fary knows your house he shall fecth it. giue him your kees with a derection wher to fiend it. [*F. K.*, ll. 1763-65]

Take prince the keys of that vnholowed place
Which doth detaine your daugthers sacred hearse. [*D. A.*, ll. 841-42]

The second class of parallels consists of verbal borrowings to fit a similar thought without regard for situation. As a few examples:

I can not I say doubt your corage being so well acquainted with your passiue fortitude. [*F. K.*, ll. 903-04]

Twas but to exercise your passive valour. [*Jealous Lovers*, I, 104]

INTRODUCTION

Confound . . . this monster. but why do I say monster? this diuil this sacrelegious diuil. [*F. K.*, ll. 919-20]

This man—said I a man?—this monster, rather—but monster is too easy a name—this devil, this incarnate devil. [*J. L.*, I, 144]

The third class consists either of paraphrases of definite passages or ideas, or of a characteristic thought or turn of phrase.

arme ye furies come to war against heauen, Ile be y^r captaine a fircer charge then ere the earth borne brood gaue to Olympus. [*F. K.*, ll. 456-57]

O, that the valiant giants would again
Rebel against the gods, and besiege heaven,
So I might be their leader. [*Muses' Looking Glass*, I, 203]

Rather condeme it to ppetual imprisment to be closely locked vp in coffers. [*F. K.*, ll. 34-35]

condemn a bag; let trash away. [*J. L.*, I, 114]

condem 2 bags of a 1000 pounds a peace. [*D. A.*, l. 144]

thos heaps of gould thou now sits brouding ouer. [*F. K.*, ll. 406-07]

And when I brooding sit upon my bags,
And every day turn o'er my heaps of gold. [*J. L.*, I, 69]

No, sit and brood on thy estate: as yet it is not hatch'd. [*M. L. G.*, I, 211]

go brode ouer your mouldy bags and hach more mony. [*D. A.*, ll. 132-33]

Hells power is contemned ye armed furies come
And ioyne with me in Chaos for to turne
Earth ayre and heauen. [*F. K.*, ll. 697-99]

What! is my power contemn'd?
Dost thou not hear my call, whose power extends
To blast the bosom of our mother Earth? [*Aristippus*, I, 3-4]

once y^o are parg'd frō the dregs of mortality. [*F. K.*, ll. 1011-12]

The fellow is a fool, and not yet purged
From his mortality. [*Amyntas*, I, 327]

being purg'd and freed from so much earth. [*Arist.*, I, 17]

Receive me, new-created of a clay
Purg'd from all dregs; my thoughts do all run clear. [*J. L.*, I, 154]

INTRODUCTION

The verbal borrowings from *The Masque of Queens* and from Shirley's *Traitor* and *Young Admiral* are appropriated almost intact from specific scenes for specific scenes in *The Fary Knight*. In contrast, with the exception of the resemblances between *The Fary Knight* and *Amyntas* (which are in the same class as those between *The Drinking Academy* and *The Jealous Lovers*), the borrowings and general paraphrases that are Randolph's occur in all his dramas and are evenly distributed throughout the play as a part of the very texture of the thought and style, not for the specific purposes of those from Jonson and Shirley. It was this wide scope plus the general style and tone that led Professor Day to ascribe *The Drinking Academy* to Randolph rather than to a plagiarist; and it is this equally wide scope in *The Fary Knight*, reenforcing Professor Day's evidence for the *Academy*, which leads a critic to distinguish between them and the Jonson-Shirley plagiarisms and to the probability that *The Fary Knight* is also Randolph's. As in *The Drinking Academy*, there is the same borrowing of incident in his other work and the consistent exhibition of stylistic peculiarities and characteristic phraseology. Randolph's habit of borrowing from himself has been exposed in detail in *The Drinking Academy*,[13] and, in part, in his other plays;[14] the self-imitation from *The Fary Knight*, therefore, is not surprising.

Certain definite characteristics set *The Fary Knight* and *The Drinking Academy* somewhat apart from the rest of Randolph's plays. His other work, in the main, is written in a rather raised "literary" style and is frequently larded with references to Cambridge and university life. There is proof that some of his plays were acted at Cambridge, and it is usually assumed that all were originally written for collegiate production, although *The Muses' Looking Glass* and *Amyntas* found their way to the London stage in 1630. By contrast, Professor Rollins notes in *The Drinking Academy* a switch to London references, a simplicity of stage settings and properties, and, most important, a limited *dramatis personæ* which contains no female character. These reasons, among others, led him to conjecture that the *Academy* was written for performance as the required English play at the Christmas festivities of

---

[13] C. L. Day, "Thomas Randolph and *The Drinking Academy*," *PMLA*, XLIII (1928), 800-7. The evidence is supplemented in the notes to *The Drinking Academy*, ed. H. E. Rollins and S. A. Tannenbaum. Since the *Academy* and *The Fary Knight* are obviously by the same author and were written in similar manuscript books by the same penman, the evidence that the *Academy* is Randolph's applies with equal force to *The Fary Knight*.

[14] G. C. Moore Smith, "The Canon of Randolph's Dramatic Works," *RES*, I (1925), 309-10; "Thomas Randolph," *Proceedings of the British Academy*, XIII (1927), 100-1. See also C. L. Day, *op. cit.*, p. 807, n. 16.

INTRODUCTION

Westminster School, which Randolph attended before his matriculation at Trinity College in July, 1624.[15] *The Fary Knight*, a longer play (at least in its revised form), expands the cast of characters slightly, but also omits women characters. Its production would be almost as simple as *The Drinking Academy*. The conjecture that the *Academy*, and therefore *The Fary Knight* as well, was written for the Westminster School is materially strengthened by the fact that *The Fary Knight* was acted by children. Craft is described as a "king of pigmies" (l. 1561) in reference to his fairy attendants, and, more important, the major character Politico is spoken of by Losserello as a "pigmey giant" (l. 1585). Before the gulling of Politico, Craft asks Snap: "Ye haue tought the children how to behaue themselues? can they do the dance?" (ll. 957-58). These words from the mouth of one who is himself a child actor point to the fairies as children considerably younger than he is. Such a gradation of age could be secured readily at a school. It is not without significance that in an inventory of school play costumes at Eton in 1570-72, among other items for the child actors is listed "ij servantes cootes for children," as distinguished from other servants' coats for the boys.[16] The play was evidently acted indoors, since Losserello in a street scene addresses the audience "under this roofe" (l. 83). The case is clinched when in the epilogue the speaker pleads,

> Our aime is at your smile if you but say
> ffalts merit pardon when as children play. [ll. 1899-1900]

The possibility that this reference is to performance by a professional children's company on the public stage is remote. Although Robert Armin in *The Two Maids of Moreclacke* (1607-08?) expressed dissatisfaction with the performance of the Children of the King's Revels, the boy actors were accustomed to plays which made infinitely greater demands on their skill than *The Fary Knight*; and such an apology from a company of professional boy actors, or from an adult company using boys, has no parallel in the whole period. The greater familiarity with the audience than in the public theaters and a corresponding intimacy in addressing it point toward a private performance (see especially ll. 54-57, 1878-81). Certain references in the Third Intermean of Jonson's *Staple of News* (1626) to conjuring in a Westminster English play are

---

[15] *The Drinking Academy*, pp. xii-xiv, xxii. For the requirement of an English play at the school, see T. H. Vail Motter, *The School Drama in England* (London, 1929), pp. 86, 88; John Sargeaunt, *Annals of Westminster School* (London, 1898), p. 49.

[16] T. H. Vail Motter, *The School Drama in England*, p. 259.

INTRODUCTION

probably to be applied to *The Fary Knight*[17] and link the play to the School. Finally, the evidence that the original version of *The Fary Knight* was probably composed for performance in 1622-24, while Randolph was attending Westminster, makes it difficult to accept a public or a university performance.[18]

VI. The Date of the Original Play

The question of the date of *The Fary Knight* is complicated by the fact that the original version of the play was materially expanded and augmented in the present manuscript. There are, therefore, two dates: one for the lost first version, which was probably by Randolph, and one for the extant final version by the unknown writer of the manuscript. Various pieces of evidence have a bearing on the date of the first production. Randolph was a precocious youth, and while still a boy of less than ten years is said to have written a *History of the Incarnation of Our Saviour*.[19] More important evidence is furnished by Richard West in "To the pious Memory of my deare Brother-in-law Mr Thomas Randolph," one of the prefatory verses to Randolph's *Poems* edited by his brother Robert in 1638. West begins:

> Readers, prepare your Fayth; who truly tells
> His History, must needs write miracles.
> Hee lisp'd Wit worthy th' Presse, as if that hee
> Had us'd his Cradle as a Librarie.

Then come four important lines:

> Some of these Fruits had birth, when other Boyes
> (His Elders) play'd with Nuts; Books were his Toyes.
> Hee had not long of Playes Spectatour beene
> But his small Feete wore Socks fit for the Scene.

---

[17] F. T. Bowers, "Ben Jonson, Thomas Randolph, and *The Drinking Academy*," *N&Q*, CLXIII (1937), 166-68.

[18] *The Fary Knight* even in its present expanded form is still rather short for presentation on the public stage, and it seems probable that in its original version it was somewhat nearer the length of the private "shows" for school and university like *The Drinking Academy*, *Aristippus*, *The Conceited Pedlar*, and probably the unexpanded forms of *The Muses' Looking Glass* and *Hey for Honesty*. But the fact that, like the first three of these plays, *The Fary Knight* employs an exclusively male cast of characters, definitely removes it from the public stage. In order to credit a college performance one would need to believe that Randolph deliberately ignored *The Alchemist*, his fundamental source, which portrayed the adult rogues pretending to be fairies, and wrote a play in which, against all collegiate custom, at least six young children were required, who were so inexpert that an apology had to be made for them. Even if this obstacle is hurdled, the fact remains that in contrast to *Aristippus* and *The Conceited Pedlar* the subject is rather "popular" and all local references to Cambridge and college life are missing.

[19] John Aubrey, *Brief Lives*, ed. Andrew Clark (Oxford, 1898), II, 192.

INTRODUCTION

That these lines refer to writing drama rather than acting in it, is shown by the fact that West continues with a discussion of Randolph as a playwright,

> Hee was not like those costive Wits, who blot
> A quire of paper to contrive a Plot.[20]

Since "small Feete" must indicate that Randolph was a schoolboy, and since he would have had the opportunity of seeing plays not only at Westminster but also on the London stage after entering school, it is by no means incredible that Randolph should write a play for his school when only sixteen to eighteen years old. And West here seems to speak directly of a play written at Westminster.

The value of the second piece of evidence may be doubtful. In lines 404-405 the usurer Covet is called "ten in the hundred," a conventional phrase for moneylenders in reference to the legal rate of interest set by Henry VIII at ten per cent. In 1624, however, a law (21 Jac. I, *c.* 17) was passed lowering the legal rate of interest to eight per cent, a change noted by various playwrights. Thus in *Wily Beguiled* (1596-1606) there is a reference to ten in the hundred (sig. A4), and in Jonson's *Every Man Out of his Humour* (1599) Carlo says of Deliro, "His wit's after ten i' the hundred" (IV. ii). By contrast, in *The Staple of News* (1626) it is remarked to Pennyboy Senior, in reference to the new law of 1624, "Your Grace be fall'n off two i' the hundred" (II. i). Rawbone in Shirley's *Wedding* (1626) asks, "What's eight in the hundred to me?" (I. iii). If this were certain evidence, there could be no hesitation in setting the date of the play in 1623 or 1624 since the act was not to take effect until June, 1625. But the phrase "ten in the hundred" may have continued proverbially without regard for the new interest rate, since it is found in Thomas May's *Old Couple* in 1636, although it must be noted that this late date is for the revision, not for the original play, which was written perhaps as early as 1619.[21] Evidence, therefore, based on this reference to usury is too uncertain to depend on for anything but general corroboration, although it need not be entirely discarded.

The probable references in the Third Intermean of *The Staple of News* to the production at Westminster of *The Fary Knight,* which

---

[20] *Poems,* ed. G. Thorn-Drury (Haslewood Books, 1929), pp. 16-17.
[21] Hazlitt's Dodsley, XII, 51. For the dating of the second version in 1636, see Alfred Harbage, *Cavalier Drama* (New York, 1936), p. 130. For the evidence in favor of an early date for the first version, see A. G. Chester, *Thomas May* (Philadelphia, 1932), pp. 76-79.

INTRODUCTION

seem to have been answered in the prologue to *The Drinking Academy*, would make Christmas of 1624 the latest date for the play, since *The Staple of News* was acted early in February, 1626. With such an approximate date in 1623 or 1624 agrees the satire on Spain which probably refers to the Spanish Marriage. Without directly mentioning the marriage, Randolph, in a manner otherwise more applicable to the early years of the century, satirizes Philip of Spain's ambitions to unite England and its empire to Spain, the infiltration of England with spies; and in the trial of Politico for aspiring to Oberon's throne it is obvious that the Spanish king is on trial for the Gunpowder Plot.[22] References to the Armada and to the Gunpowder Plot were commonplaces even at this late date, but not in the form of the detailed satire found in *The Fary Knight*. An audience at Christmas of 1623 or 1624 would not, however, have been slow to recognize the pointed shafts at the danger of allying England with a nation which had earlier made attempts on its territory and religion.

Strong evidence for a date in the 1620's is furnished in ll. 541-42. Losserello, impatient to be enchanted, has expressed surprise that the Devil is such a drinker. Covet gives as the result of the Devil's liquorish thirst: "what do y° thinke makes so many vintners breake in the City but his vngodly gut that feches of whole hogsheads at a draught?" This jesting reason for the financial difficulties of vintners probably refers to their serious embarrassment following the advance in the price of wines in 1621-22, 1623-24, or 1624-25, perhaps in combination with the severe penalties enacted in James's perpetuation of the Act against Drunkenness (21 Jac. I, *c.* 7) in 1623-24. The scarcity and dearness of wine following the rise in prices is mentioned in almost identical language in the anonymous *Wine, Beere, Ale, and Tobacco*, a Cambridge play of about 1624-26: "But thou art come down of late to a glasse, Wine; and that's the reason I thinke, so many Vintners haue broake" (ll. 325-26).[23] It is probably indicative of the new state of affairs that Spendall, even though he is a prodigal, is drinking "glaces" of wine in *The Fary Knight* (l. 282) instead of pots.

In lines 60-63 Craft remarks, "In this ruffe I looke like Hanse van Verking Snort burgar master of Amsterdame newly arriued in Ingland with a brace of Holland Cheses to bribe the new states that ould ones might haue time to louse them selues." Between 1620 and 1660 there

---
[22] See ll. 161-71, 225-26, 264-66, 1555-56, 1643 ff.
[23] "Wine, Beere, Ale, and Tobacco," ed. J. H. Hanford, *Studies in Philology*, XII (1915), 7, 40, 48.

INTRODUCTION

were four burgomasters of Amsterdam who visited England on missions: (1) Reynier Pauw, who in 1613 was delegated with Hugo de Groot to James I by the High Powers of the Netherlands in the interest of the East India Company, and who was knighted by James on February 12, 1621; (2) Dr. Dirck Bas, Knight, and his commission, from December 5, 1621, to February 12, 1623; (3) Dr. Gerard Schaep and his commission from December 15, 1651, to June 30, 1652; (4) Simon van Hoorn, Ambassador Extraordinary, with Louys van Nassau, Michiel van Gogh, and Joachim Ripperda, who were assigned to the court of Charles II in 1660. Of these four, either Bas or Schaep is almost certainly the subject of the reference. Dr. Gerard Schaep and two companions, Van de Perre and Cats, came to England in 1651 to complain of the seizure of Dutch ships under letters of reprisal against either Holland or France, and also to work for the repeal of the Navigation Act. They were joined by Pauw on June 5, but the ill-feeling in England against Admiral Tromp for his attack on Blake, and in Holland for the continued seizure of Dutch ships by the English, nullified all hopes for reconciliation, and the ambassadors departed on June 30, 1652, before the outbreak of the war. If Schaep is the person referred to, the lines were probably written in 1651-52 and by the transcriber of the manuscript. While part of the pun would be clear, in that "new states" could mean the English Commonwealth and "ould ones" the United Provinces, the reference to bribery and to delousing remains obscure in relation to Schaep's mission.

On the other hand, a reasonable meaning can be gained as applied to Dirck Bas. Bas was the most prominent of his commission of three since he was the chief director of the Dutch East Indies Company and his appointment was obnoxious to the English, who considered him too personally involved to act as a disinterested arbiter. He had gained his office by some chicanery involving charges of bribery, and he acted with considerable arrogance in England. English commissioners had been sent to him in Holland in 1618-19 to negotiate, but the agreement reached was so unsatisfactory that there were allegations of bribery when the commissioners returned to England with excessively rich gifts from the Dutch. The general reference, then, seems to be to the bribery of the fresh set of English commissioners or "new states" whom Bas is now meeting, so that the "old states" (either the states concerned in the old quarrel or the former set of commissioners who had failed) may now be at peace, with past failures forgotten.

INTRODUCTION

"Holland Cheses" probably refers to Bas's two companions, but may be a satirical reference to gifts brought from Amsterdam to smooth his way. The commissioners from Holland were received in public audience by James on January 6, 1622; negotiations started February 16, 1622, but did not conclude until February of 1623.[24] The word "newly," however, had no connotation of especial immediacy in the seventeenth century, and the allusion could well have been written over a year or two after 1622 when negotiations were proceeding.

The probable date for *The Fary Knight* may, therefore, be set at Christmas of 1622-24, with perhaps a preference for 1623-24.[25] With this dating agree West's testimony that Randolph wrote plays while still a schoolboy, the generalized satire on the Spanish Marriage, the change in the usury rates from ten to eight per cent in 1624-25, the rise in the price of wines and James's Act against Drunkenness, Jonson's jests in *The Staple of News* about a conjuring play at Westminster, and the probable reference to the arrival of Dirck Bas. The apparent order of composition by which *The Fary Knight* seems to precede *Amyntas* must also be taken into account.

VII. The Status of the Manuscript

The date 1623-24 can hold only for the original composition and production of *The Fary Knight*, since the manuscript is not Randolph's own and it exhibits signs of revisions and augmentations which cannot be Randolph's. It is time to consider this aspect of the problem. The borrowings from *The Traitor* (1631, published 1635) are confined chiefly to the elaboration of the trial of Politico in the final scene, and there is no difficulty in assuming that they expanded a shorter and more elementary incident in the original. Indeed, slight confirmation is found in the trial in *The Jealous Lovers* (IV. iv), which seems to have

---

[24] *Calendar of State Papers, Venetian (1621-23)*, pp. xxx ff., 138, 141, 173, 197, 563; see also under Dirck (or Thierry) Bas: *Calendar of State Papers Colonial East Indies (1617-21)*; *Calendar of State Papers Colonial East Indies (1622-24)*.

[25] It cannot be determined whether there is any connection between the manuscript *The Fary Knight* and the licensing to the Prince's company in Herbert's books on June 11, 1624, of a play *The Fairy Knight* by Thomas Dekker and John Ford. One fact, at any rate, is clear. The borrowings from *The Young Admiral*, not licensed until 1633, prevent any possibility that the Folger manuscript represents the lost Dekker-Ford play. *The Fary Knight* is not suited for the popular stage and there are no reasonable signs of the work of Dekker or of Ford in the play which could possibly lead to the view that the manuscript represents a revision of their work. If *The Fairy Knight* by Dekker and Ford was concerned with Huon of Bordeaux, as has been conjectured, the professional play may have provided the amateur writer of *The Fary Knight* with some inspiration for his burlesque of the Huon story. If this were so, then we could set the date definitely at Christmas, 1624. For the Dekker-Ford play, see F. G. Fleay, *A Biographical Chronicle*, I, 232, E. K. Chambers, *The Elizabethan Stage*, III, 304.

INTRODUCTION

borrowed slightly from *The Fary Knight*. Plagiarism from *The Young Admiral*, however, at first sight seems to strike at the very foundation of the plot concerning Losserello. In *The Young Admiral* (III. i) Didimo promises to make Pazzorello invulnerable so that he may prove a brave soldier; and in IV. i, with the help of Flavia disguised as a witch, Pazzorello is charmed. In *The Alchemist*, *The Fary Knight*, and *The Young Admiral* the gull is pinched by supposed supernatural beings and is forced to empty his pockets before the incantation.

That the writer of the Folger manuscript, and not Shirley, was the borrower is indicated by the manner in which one phrase in *The Fary Knight* can be explained only by reference to *The Young Admiral*. Losserello has failed to intimidate Politico by his threats and says (l. 1419), "Nay then I must fight tho it be but for my hanches." These words are meaningless unless we refer to *The Young Admiral* (III. i) where Didimo is describing to Pazzorello the dangers of the *perdu:* "Or, if he fight, to be cut into honourable collops, or [have] his limbs strewed about the field, which found by a sutler's wife, are sod for the knapsack-men, and go current for camp mutton." Pazzorello is not enticed by the prospect that his body may be boiled for eating, and demands, in a speech that explains the phrase in *The Fary Knight*, "Have the bullets first salute me, lie *perdu*, as you call it, and be cut into honourable collops, or have my haunches sod by a sutler's wife, and pass for camp mutton! this is the preferment you wish me to, master Didimo?"[26]

In view of the fundamental means and motives in the enchantments of Losserello and Pazzorello, the question may be raised whether the entire character of Losserello, his enchantment and fight with Politico, were not added later. The original *Fary Knight* would thus have been a simple "show," close in length to *The Drinking Academy*, and con-

[26] So, by analogy, it may seem that the writer of *The Fary Knight* manuscript was also the borrower from *The Traitor*. Some corroboration is given by the rather rare phrase "rat of Nilus" which is used by no other dramatist of the period except Shirley and this writer. This phrase was borrowed as a part of the trial scene from *The Traitor*, but it occurs, in addition, earlier in *The Fary Knight*. The inference may follow that the writer took this previous use also from *The Traitor* rather than from Shirley's *Love Tricks* (1625). That the writer of the manuscript and not Randolph (in some hypothetical revision of his own early play later copied by the writer) was the borrower from Shirley's *Young Admiral* at least, is apparent, since the borrowings are too close to have been made from hearing the play, and *The Young Admiral* was not published until 1637, two years after Randolph's death. It is possible, but improbable, that Randolph had the manuscripts of the two Shirley plays before him in such a hypothetical revision (*The Traitor* was published in 1635), but such a theory is complex indeed. The very definite evidence that at least some of the borrowings from *The Masque of Queens* were made during the writing of the manuscript, combined with some slight signs of composition in the borrowings from *The Traitor*, may well lead to the view that both the Shirley plays were also laid under contribution by the writer and not by Randolph.

INTRODUCTION

sisting only in the gulling of Politico and Covet, with a conflict between Politico and Spendall, and finally a scene at the end where Politico is crowned and the cheat exposed. There are, however, reasons for believing that Losserello was present in the original cast of characters as a gull tricked by a cheating incantation. Firstly, only on the assumption of an enchantment scene employing witches and the devil in *The Fary Knight* can the allusions be explained in *The Staple of News* in 1626, and the prologue to *The Drinking Academy*, in answer, be consistently unraveled. Secondly, the confusion that exists in *The Fary Knight* about Losserello's aspirations tends more to the view that he was originally present in the play but may have undergone certain revisory changes. Craft, for example, first promises him the reversion of Oberon's throne, just as he later promises Politico. The invulnerability incident is introduced because Losserello must kill a giant in order to prove himself worthy of succeeding Oberon. Yet at the end Losserello has no protest when Politico is elevated to the throne, and is quite content with the title of Oberon's fairy knight. Thirdly, various of Randolph's plays seem to have been influenced by, rather than to have influenced, *The Fary Knight*. Given *The Alchemist*, *Huon of Bordeaux*, and perhaps Fletcher's *Women Pleased*, the action and character of Losserello and his yearning to be a fairy knight are complete as the fundamental basis of the play. On the contrary, the fairy knight Jocastus in *Amyntas* (1630) is not an integral part of the plot and his conception can be traced by no such straight paths as Losserello's except on the inference that he is modeled after Losserello. In every turn of the gulling, Jocastus is a paler copy. Correspondingly, the witch and fury disguises in *The Drinking Academy* stem rather from their natural employment in *The Fary Knight* than from *The Alchemist*.

Fourthly, a close examination of the scene of Losserello's enchantment seems to reveal an original version overlaid by later borrowings. The scene starts with a conversation about the devil and wine (ll. 530 ff.) which appears to be Randolph's own.[27] With the entrance of Craft and the witch (ll. 573 ff.) the borrowings from Shirley begin with Losserello's presentation. The discussion about the money on Losserello's person and his fleecing is borrowed about equally from Shirley and *The Alchemist* with verbal resemblances to both. The verse charms before the final anointing are practically uninfluenced by Shirley, al-

---

[27] The reference to the breaking of vintners (ll. 541-42) is to events in the mid-1620's or slightly before. See p. xxxi, above.

INTRODUCTION

though the comic prose interjections are from *The Young Admiral*. The first charm is almost entirely original, with some influence from Ovid; the second and third the same with some general details from either *The Masque of Queens* or Lucan. The close verbal paraphrase or outright borrowing from *The Masque of Queens* begins in the continuation of the third charm (ll. 713 ff.) and continues through the appearances of the various witches to their dance (l. 823). Thereupon the scene concludes with the comic anointing from Shirley and some borrowings from *The Alchemist*.

The changes made by the writer of the manuscript throughout this scene show it to have been the most revised in the play during the actual course of the transcribing. Ll. 713-14, for instance, were a revision in paraphrase of two deleted lines direct from *The Masque of Queens*, and were made before the succeeding lines were written. Ll. 798-99 were taken over almost verbatim from Jonson when the writer realized the preceding couplet (which he deleted) was a repetition of the words assigned earlier (ll. 789-90) to another witch and probably part of the original version. Ll. 761-67 were later added vertically on the page when the writer found he needed music for the dance of the witches first mentioned in ll. 822-23.

Thus, although borrowings from Shirley had nothing to do with the actual series of charms, there was patent revision from Jonson's *Masque of Queens* made at the time of writing. On the other hand, this Jonsonian revision through verbal borrowing is not at all present in the first charm, and only slightly in the second. When these two charms are examined apart from the others, various differences immediately appear. The first charm, the most original, is cast in vaguely classical terms in contrast to the definiteness of the items in the rest. Its last line, "Wee'l make him sone as mad as we be," introduces a burlesque note not present in the actual charms of Jonson or Shirley. The start of the second charm (ll. 669-74),

> Come ye gobblings that do creepe
> Throught dores when the maids are aslepe,
> Bring the entrels of the rat
> With the mewings of the cat.
> Ye nimble ffaunes and siluans all
> Be not absent at our call,

is based on fairy rather than witch lore, on white magic rather than black, and contrasts sharply with the tone of the borrowings. The orig-

INTRODUCTION

inal scene seems to have retained most of the fairy atmosphere of *The Alchemist* on which it was founded. Craft earlier promises Losserello that Oberon wishes him to be carried "to my grannams a fary wich whos spel will make you so impregnable" (ll. 148-49). Hecate cries (ll. 691-92),

> Ile speake a charme
> Shall make the faries rise from depest hell,

and later uses an innocuous charm "Triphon Cocabel Camas" (l. 717) with its fairy names to raise the devil. On the evidence of ll. 798-99, which show Jonsonian lines introduced as a substitute, it would seem that most of the borrowings from *The Masque of Queens* were probably introduced in company with those from *The Young Admiral* in the augmentation of the original scene based on, and borrowing from, *The Alchemist*.

It becomes important, therefore, to ascertain whether Randolph could have formed the character Losserello and the enchantment scene before the appearance of *The Young Admiral*. The enchantment of the heroes of romances was a commonplace and is mentioned by Craft as a parallel to what he is proposing: "Was not s^r Amides de Gall and Don Sel del Phæbo both of them inchanted and by virteu of ther spell did feats nations stod a tiptoo to heare of" (ll. 153-55). Losserello responds (ll. 156-57): "O I remember! what a blockehead am I, I an s^r Huen of Burdox and the blacke prince were both of them enchanted." In Jonson's *Every Man Out of his Humour* (IV. ii) Puntarvolo promises, "Neither shall I use the help of any such sorceries, or enchantments, as unctions to make our skins impenetrable." Albumazar gives Pandolfo a magic cap and image (I. viii):

> With these walk as unwounded as Achilles
> Dipp'd by his mother Thetis.

In Fletcher's *Women Pleased* (IV. ii) a lady in the likeness of a witch causes her gallant to become valiant in battle by tricking him into the belief that her influence will make him invincible. The romance *Huon of Bordeaux*, from which a lost play was made as early as 1593, portrays Oberon adopting a knight and making him heir to fairyland. The Dekker-Ford *Fairy Knight* in 1624 may have offered various suggestions. Ariosto's *Orlando Furioso* (canto xxix) introduces a scene based on the belief in magic invulnerability.

INTRODUCTION

Randolph, therefore, had no need for Shirley to point the way. The germ of *The Fary Knight* and the gulling of Losserello and Politico came direct from *Huon of Bordeaux* and from *The Alchemist*, where the Fairy Queen promised Dapper thousands of acres in Fairyland. As Dol vowed that Dapper would be her favorite, so Losserello is to ingratiate himself as Oberon's favorite by slaying a giant. His head is full of old romances, the heroes of which he has taken as models. His charm is to be not a lucky gambling "fly" but one that will make him victorious against giants like the knights of old. As in *The Alchemist* the enchantment scene was originally dominated by a fairy atmosphere, in all likelihood, and the victorious charm was spun over Losserello by Craft's fairy witch, who roused the devil, and probably various subsidiary witches, to her aid by charms loosely combining fairy lore with infernal allusions drawn from Ovid and Lucan.

The status of the writer of the Folger and Huntington manuscripts can now be estimated. When in 1928 Professor Day surveyed the evidence of style and incident linking *The Drinking Academy* to Randolph's acknowledged plays, particularly the influence of *The Drinking Academy* on *The Jealous Lovers* and the outright borrowings made from the *Academy* by the later play, the inference was inevitable that the *Academy* was either the work of an extremely servile plagiarist of Randolph, or of Randolph himself. The wide scope of the borrowings plus the similarity in style and tone led him to conclude that Randolph was indeed the author.[28] No stronger case for Randolph could have been presented outside of the appearance of his name on the title-page or the establishment of the manuscript as a Randolph holograph; and Professor Moore Smith, the eminent authority on Randolph, reviewed Professor Day's claim for Randolph with approval, provided only that the date of the play were set later than 1625 and that Randolph were not considered the actual writer of the manuscript.[29] When on all the evidence then available Professor Rollins and Dr. Tannenbaum in their edition declared the manuscript holographic, since the signs of actual composition and revision apparently by an author seemed to outweigh the fact that the writing bore no resemblance to the two signatures of Randolph, which could be in a formalized hand, Professor Moore Smith felt impelled to forsake his original views in favor of Professor Day's discarded alternative of a servile plagiarist. Even though Robert Baron

---

[28] C. L. Day, *PMLA*, XLIII (1928), 800-09.
[29] G. C. Moore Smith, *PMLA*, XLIV (1929), 631-33.

INTRODUCTION

can no longer be viewed as the plagiarist author of the play,[30] the original cause for the cleavage in points of view has remained unresolved.

The recent authentication in Dr. W. W. Greg's *English Literary Autographs* of a small amount of Randolph's handwriting (which coincides with the writing of the signatures as evidence that the signatures are not formalized compositions), and the discovery of the similarity of the manuscripts of *The Drinking Academy* and *The Fary Knight*, have provided sufficient additional evidence to approach the problem with more confidence. The paradox of alterations apparently by a composing and revising author combined with a non-holographic manuscript is to be solved by the evidence contained only in *The Fary Knight* that a writer who is far from being a mere scribal copyist is revising and augmenting an earlier manuscript as he transcribes it. That this earlier manuscript was an original play by Thomas Randolph is most probable from the scope and type of the borrowings as well as from general style, characterization, and dramatic treatment: all buttressed by Professor Day's strong case for *The Drinking Academy*. Nor is an example lacking of similar treatment accorded another Randolph play. Randolph's *Hey for Honesty* had apparently sunk from view and might not have come down to us in any form if one F. J. had not taken it in hand, enlarged it with a considerable amount of his own writing, and printed it in 1651 as "Translated out of Aristophanes his Plutus, by Tho: Randolph. Augmented and Published by F. J." As another possible parallel the Latin *Cornelianum Dolium* may represent a lost Randolph comedy, perhaps in English, reworked by another writer.[31]

Such a theory answers every objection to Randolph's authorship of *The Fary Knight* and *The Drinking Academy*, and is backed by at least one other example of the similar treatment of a Randolph play. Correspondingly, the evidence in *The Fary Knight* is strong against a plagiarist. In situation, the conception of Dorylas and Jocastus in *Amyntas* comes from *The Fary Knight* and not direct from *The Alchemist*. As to language, the borrowings from *The Masque of Queens* and from Shirley's *Traitor* and *Young Admiral* are appropriated by the augmenter from specific scenes for specific purposes. In contrast, with the exception of the borrowings between *The Fary Knight* and *Amyntas*, the borrowings and general paraphrases that are Randolph's occur in

---

[30] G. C. Moore Smith, *RES*, VI (1930), 476-83; H. E. Rollins, *PMLA*, XLVI (1931), 786-801.
[31] G. C. Moore Smith, "The Canon of Randolph's Dramatic Works," *RES*, I (1925), 315.

INTRODUCTION

all his dramas and are evenly distributed throughout the play as a part of the very texture of his thought and style, not for the specific purposes of those from Jonson and Shirley. It was this similar wide scope plus the general style and tone that led Professor Day to ascribe *The Drinking Academy* to Randolph rather than to a plagiarist, and motivated Professor Moore Smith's original approval:

> It is hard to imagine a plagiarist borrowing phrases of Randolph's from a number of different sources. . . . If *The Drinking Academy* is the work of anyone but Randolph, its date must be much later than the date which other evidence suggests. . . . Accordingly, in spite of some difficulties, I accept Mr. Day's view that *The Drinking Academy* was written by Randolph some years before *The Jealous Lovers*.[32]

So with *The Fary Knight*. To visualize a plagiarist of Randolph as its author, one would be forced to accept the hypothesis that this plagiarist wrote an original play about 1622-24 (since the evidence for a date in the early 1620's cannot be ignored) and then over fifteen years later revised his work by pilfering from Randolph, Shirley, and Jonson, with the whole under the influence of Randolph, the least noteworthy playwright of the three.

The identity of the augmenter of Randolph's work responsible for the manuscripts of *The Fary Knight* and *The Drinking Academy* is unknown. It would be sheer guesswork to ascribe them to the F. J. of *Hey for Honesty*, and neither manuscript play contains the Commonwealth allusions which are sprinkled so plentifully through *Hey for Honesty*. On the dangerous basis of the initials, this F. J. has been conjecturally identified with the Francis Jaques, whose manuscript play *The Queen of Corsica* is preserved in British Museum MS. Lansdowne 807. A comparison of the handwriting of *The Fary Knight* with the writing of this manuscript, which is presumably Jaques's holograph, discloses no points of similarity. Jaques's name is not in the registers of either Cambridge or Oxford, and it seems probable that the writer of *The Fary Knight* was, or had been, a member of Cambridge since he borrows from Peter Hausted's Cambridge play *The Rival Friends* (1632).

The extent of the writer's revision of Randolph's original play can be determined within certain limits. Unless the excessively complicated hypothesis be held that Randolph had revised his early play with bor-

---

[32] G. C. Moore Smith, *PMLA*, XLIV (1929), 631-32.

INTRODUCTION

rowings from the manuscript of *The Young Admiral* after its production in July, 1633,[33] most of the comic prose in Losserello's enchantment and some of the dialogue in his combat with Politico must have been added by the augmenter. The augmenter, unless a somewhat earlier revision by Randolph is to be credited, also made the borrowings from *The Traitor* to expand Politico's trial. The evidence is clear that at least part of the borrowings from Jonson's *Masque of Queens* was made by the writer of the manuscript, although it is possible that this masque had exercised some influence on Randolph's version of Losserello's enchantment.[34] The augmenter apparently made the few slight borrowings from Peter Hausted's *Rival Friends*.[35] There is no evidence (although the theory is quite possible) to show that the augmenter added any part of the plot, or any entire scene, not present in Randolph's version. What can be adduced is that he amplified certain key scenes.

The expansion of the dialogue made by the writer outside of these important and lengthy borrowings from Jonson and Shirley is largely a matter of conjecture. Craft's description of fairyland to Politico remains the longest original augmentation that can be identified with any confidence. Other expansions in the text that can be recognized are invariably short and unimportant. A close study of the play leads to the conviction that, as a general rule, the writer contented himself with following his manuscript. The text, so far as can be determined, is peppered with small revisions of individual words and phrases and very occasionally of whole sentences, but with the exception of the major expansions already detailed, it is probable that it remains substantially Randolph's.

One can only guess at the writer's purpose in revising these two plays. It is possible, but not probable, that the manuscripts represent a revision

---

[33] That Randolph could have revised his early play at this late date is by no means impossible. The prefatory matter to his published plays contains references to his revisions before publication, and the manuscripts of *Aristippus* and *The Conceited Pedlar* when compared to the published text attest to this practice. But the fact that Randolph or his literary executor Robert Randolph did not publish *The Fary Knight* or *The Drinking Academy* is some slight evidence that no such revision took place. More important, *The Masque of Queens* was certainly used for augmentation in *The Fary Knight*.

[34] There is no positive evidence for this statement except slight indications that parts of the scene which the editor believes untouched by the augmenter betray a general influence. Nothing, of course, would be more probable. Once Randolph altered the fairies of *The Alchemist* to fairy witches, Jonson's masque would furnish him with various ready-made details for his charms, and he was likely to go to Jonson for his precedents.

[35] The relation between *The Fary Knight* and *The Rival Friends* is not certain. Partly because the gulling of Stipes in *The Rival Friends* seems to come from *Amyntas* rather than from *The Fary Knight*, and partly because one must believe that Randolph revised his play after 1632 if it was he who borrowed from Hausted, it is the editor's opinion that Hausted did not know *The Fary Knight* and that it was the augmenter who borrowed from Hausted.

INTRODUCTION

after Randolph's death in March, 1635, for further school performance. If one knew anything about F. J. and his reasons for reworking *Hey for Honesty* from a university "show," one could conjecture with more confidence. It might be guessed that a university acquaintance of Randolph secured the manuscripts. He fancied himself as an amateur writer and either for his private amusement, as a literary exercise, or more probably from a desire to refurbish for publishing in Randolph's name and his own, two somewhat immature and early plays, like the unknown F. J. of *Hey for Honesty* he took the pains to transcribe the manuscripts with his own improvements.[36]

Thomas Randolph is steadily climbing in critical esteem. *The Fary Knight*, unfortunately, will hardly add to his reputation as a dramatist, but it has been a pleasure to recover a manuscript, even though revised by another writer, of a play which probably represents Randolph's earliest known attempt at the dramatic form.[37]

---

[36] The manuscript's lost epitaph on Frances Monson, whose country seat in Northorpe, Lincolnshire, was only fifteen miles from Barnetby le Wold, a living held at the time of her death by Thomas Randolph's brother and literary executor Robert Randolph, presents a certain problem. It would be very tempting, following this hint, to conjecture that the writer of the plays was Robert; but unfortunately the handwriting bears no resemblance to the various specimens of Robert's signature and regular hand in the parish registers. The loss of the epitaph and devotional verse and prose makes conjecture futile, but it is still possible to guess that the writer of this lost matter may have been Robert. One slight piece of evidence, however, may possibly point in the opposite direction. *The Drinking Academy* originally began with a blank leaf, recto and verso. At some date after the completion of the manuscript, the writer added in the light brown ink used for corrections in the text an Epigram on the Synod of Dort on the recto of this blank page. If the conjecture is correct that the *Academy* was originally bound in the same volume as *The Fary Knight*, the fact that this epigram seems to have no connection with the *Academy* might possibly indicate that the writer was using up blank pages in the complete manuscript volume for literary efforts of a miscellaneous nature. Hence it might follow that the writer of the epigram and of the epitaph was the same person. But since this whole matter is so highly conjectural, it is safe to assert only that the epitaph serves to link the volume with Thomas Randolph through its possible connection either with his brother or with a Lincolnshire friend of Robert Randolph.

[37] *The Drinking Academy* is probably to be dated as approximately 1626. See F. T. Bowers, *The Huntington Library Quarterly*, I (1938), 190-92.

THE FARY KNIGHT
OR
OBERON THE SECOND

<2—2—0>

[Fol. 1]   The ffary Knight∼
                            Or∼
                    Oberon the Second∼

                     The Speakers∼

Politico a foolish politision and moke King of ffaries	[5]
Loserello the ffairy Knight.	
Spendall a Prodigal	
Couet a vserer	
Craft a Cheater	
Snap and Shift his seruants	[10]
Wiches ⎫ persons asumed by Craft and his companians to	
Diuil ⎬ perfect their cheat.	
ffaries ⎭	
Oliuer ⎫	
Lansprosade ⎬ seruants	[15]
Drummer ⎭	
Vintners	
Barresters	
Elues	
Iudges &c:	[20]

[Fol. 1ᵛ]   The Prologue∼

Not in heigh numbers we intend to bring
The fates of Princes in a labored scene.
Wee seeke not with tragicke euents to fright,
Or to affect you with a sad delight.   [5]
Our aime is laughter, if we that do moue
It will a garland to our labours proue.
How euer Sirs our deuty we will pay,
And beg your kind acceptance of our Play.

DRAMATIS PERSONÆ

[Fol. 1]

  5 *moke*] *k* written over what seems to be a *c* before the final *e* was written
 10 *his*] dark brown ink over *their*
 11-12 *persons asumed . . . cheat.*] added later with the bracket in the light brown ink
 12 *their*] dk. br. ink over *his*
 15 *seruants*] added in the lt. br. ink; final *s* heavily mended

TEXTUAL NOTES

[Fol. 1ᵛ]

  3 *labored*] written over *elaborat*

THE FARY KNIGHT

[Fol. 2] *Actus primus*~

Scæna 1ᵃ~

Enter Couet and Spendal~

Couet You'l seale the writings?
Spen   Seale them Couet? Ile seale them and seale them.
       may I neuer see day of pleasure if I intend to cousen
       thee.
Coue: You are more noble sir.
Spen   I value no more land then I do dirt. it is not all the
       akers the great Magul is master of I wold exchange
       an howers pleasure for. I esteme not thy gould Couet but
       as a meanes to my pleasure.
Couet Care you not for gould sir? (O prodigie!) Ile furnish you
       with siluer. good faith I had rather do it.
Spen: No Couet it is all but drosse. whole India in my iudgments bal
       lance is out waid by a dram of pleasure. pleasure is able to
       make men immortal and turne a 100 and 10 to 15. O deare
       pleasure I do hugge the.
Coue: But what will gould do sir?
Spen: It is an enemy to pleasure. it will make him miserable
       that Reepes it.
Coue: What then intend you with that I must pay you for your
       land?~
[Fol. 2ᵛ] Spen: Exercise my rage vpon it and spend it.
Coue: Rather condeme it to ppetual imprisnmt to be closely locked
       vp in coffers and let me be iaylor.
Spen: No Couet it is to slight a punishment for so greuious an offen
       der. Ile to court to the Diuil tauerne, where sentance of ppe
       tual banishment frõ our trunkes and pockets shall iuridically
       be pronounced against this friend of care and arch traitor of
       pleasure. Couet fare wel my boy shall be the apparitor
       to sommon the malefactor frõ the prison in thy house thy
       mouldy bagges and coffers to appeare at the tauerne barre
       ther to receaue condigne punishment.   Exit

[Fol. 2]
15 *see*] final *e* apparently altered from *a*
18 *dirt*] *t* altered from some illegible letter
19 *akers*] *k* altered from *c*, apparently before *ers* was written
24 *is*] interlined above a caret in dk. br. ink
26 *and turne*] *and* over an erasure; a *t* faintly discernible under the *n*

27 *hugge*] the second *g* apparently altered from an illegible letter which may be *e*
29 *enemy*] *y* altered from dotted *i*

[Fol. 2ᵛ]
35 *iaylor*] a final letter, apparently an *s*, erased, after which the *r* was mended
38 *pockets*] *t* altered from *d*

THE FARY KNIGHT

Coue: Monster of men! and thinks thou that I for all thy land will
be guilty of so sacrelegious a crime as to send goulden angels to [45]
the diuil for so he termed that profane place the tauerne
where my beloued gould must receaue sentence, as he sayed, of per
petual banishment. no, no it is piety to cossen him. Ile home
and make it my study how to hold from him his land yet keepe
my gold~   Exit   [50]

Scæna 2ª

Enter Craft~

Craf: It begins to worke. Couet Ile be with thee anon and you M^r
Spendall shall haue my company. I may chance sirs to rayes
your admiration concerning my person. for as you se I can [55]
Lady like change my fashon. this venerable beard speaks me
a spaniard. for looke now in my face and se if you do not espie an 88
[an 88] Armado or a fleat of gould sailing frõ the Indies in my
[Fol. 3] forehead. faith Ile be honest with you, you shall se all. in this
ruffe I looke like Hanse van Verking Snort burgar master of [60]
Amsterdame newly arriued in Ingland with a brace of Holland
Cheses to bribe the new states that ould ones might haue time to
louse them selues. I wold shew you a french man but to do that
feat I shold haue an exchange in my briches to furnish me with
variety of formes. I beleue you guesse at my profession allre [65]
ady, neuerthe lesse vpon promise of y^r future silence Ile in
forme y^o more. I am a Marcury brought vp in the citie,
a land fisher that diues in euery ones pocket. I was trained vp
by the most exquisit of the trade, and serued my prenteshipe
in newgate. yet sinse I thanke my stars aduanced to heigher [70]
preferment, fortune hath made me master of a company, and
now I haue men to do for me what I was wont to do [for] my selfe
but [notwt] not withstanding I must like Æsops cat follow
my old course of hunting. whist who comes heere a prise
I hope.~   *he steps aside*   [75]

---

45 *so*] interlined above a caret in the lt. br. ink
57 *an 88*] added in the margin in the lt. br. ink
58 [*an 88*]] *88* interlined above a caret and later deleted in the lt. br. ink; still later *an* deleted in the dk. br. ink and another stroke in this ink made across *88*

[Fol. 3]
70 *sinse*] initial *s* over some illegible letter

72 [*for*] *my*] *for* blotted heavily and probably intended to be deleted
73 [*notwt*]] the writer apparently made a *w* and then a *t*, but there is a dot over the third minim of the *w*
74 *heere*] the second *e* mended and perhaps altered from *a*
75 *hope.*] the following decoration deletes some illegible letters

THE FARY KNIGHT

Scæna 3ª

Enter Losserello~

Loss O that I had bin borne in king Arthurs dayes, when honour
went a begging, and euery round table knight had her for his
Zane. the world was then full of dragons, enchanted castles [80]

[Fol. 3ᵛ] and ladies and euery lousy knight was able to kil you his
giant of a 1000 miles in compasse when now adayes ther
are as braue spirits to be found and tho' I say it vnder this roofe.
but because ther are no dragons or giants to kill they scearse de
serue to haue ther names in blacke and white but in a tauerne bill [85]
or on the backe side of an old Almanicke for debt. O tempora
O moribus! shall Gie of Worricks cow æternize his name and in
rich the states with mony for the history of a deade euery bucher
can æqual him in whilst such a valior as burnes in this breast
is neglected? I cold mutany for angre. who comes here? O that [90]
it were a Giant as great as Magolet whom Sir Tristram
slew in farelands~

Scena 4ª enter Craft blowing a horne

~[Shifte]~~~~~

Craf Twiue, Twiue tan twiue: blesse me my stars! Mars is
in his height and with his glorious raise displayed vpon this [95]
place most historicaly tels the prodegy of valuor to be at
hand for whom the illustrious Oberon hath sough Africke Asia
and 3 parts of America~

Los: It is not me he meanes is it?

Craf: By the stygian lacke that stately posture he walkes in was]100
a marke King Oberon gaue me to know him by.

Loss: Nay then I se it is me he lookes for: I will vse more heroicke
gestures~

[Fol. 4] Craf by the fary sceptor I discouer the influence of the 7 stars
in his forehead and plainely se the spot one his eye lid que [105]
ne Mab left to know him by when she kist him in his cra

[Fol. 3ᵛ]
87 *cow*] interlined above a caret
89 *valior*] the *i* in the dk. br. ink over what may be a *u*; the *a* very closely resembles an *o*
89 *burnes*] as the writer was forming a *t* he altered it to *b*; the loop was later mended in the lt. br. ink to make the letter clearer
91 *Sir*] S altered in the dk. br. ink from an illegible letter, probably *s*
93 The decoration below this line deletes *Shifte*

94 *stars!*] the exclamation mark added in the lt. br. ink
94 *Mars*] M altered from *m* in the dk. br. ink
94 *is*] added in the margin in the lt. br. ink
95 *height*] *t* added in the lt. br. ink
100 *stygian*] *y* altered from dotted *i*

[Fol. 4]
106 *cra*] *a* altered from *e*

THE FARY KNIGHT

            dle. Ile accost him. most heroicke sir daine a mortal the
            priuiligd to kisse that hand the faites haue decreed shall hould the
            ball of the fary empire.
Los: It is a fauour I denie kings but because I perceaue y͠o are   [110]
            a stranger come frõ the fairy court Ile grant you the prero
            gatiue.
Craft   Thanks most excellent prince for this ambrosian kisse worth
            more land then Cam can call his. O heauens! all   ⎡*he lookes*
                                  [the lines of hap
            pines concenter heare. I thought sir your glory   *vpon his* [115]
                                  [wold haue bin con
            find with in the limits of ffary land. but now I   *hand*
                                  [plainely see ⎣
            it will streach it selfe from pole to pole. the world will be to lit
            tle for your greatnes.
Los: But art sure of this?
Craft   Sure? am I sure I liue? am I sure I kisse your Royal hand? [120]
            it is mere infidelitie to doubt it. that vaine in your forehead
            is a certaine signe in palmistry the world shall not se y^r [ou] eqal.
            fame shall forget the deads of Alixander and fil her goulden trum
            pet only with y^r name.
Loss: Rise vp rise vp thou shalt knele no longer for thy goode newes. [125]
            by this light I might haue vewed my selfe ouer and ouer in a
            looking glasse and not haue discouered halfe the good fortune
            you tel me of. but dost come frõ fary-land and art sent by
            Oberon to find me out?
Craf: I am most illustrious prince.   [130]
[Fol. 4^v] Loss: Harke he cals me prince to.
Craf: My great master Oberon implores your aid.
Los: My aide, what to do?
Craf: To kil a tirrible giant in his dominians that [deuors] deuoers men
            and beasts.   [135]
Los: Men and [beatss] beasts? by this light Ile haue no thing to do with
            him. I [that] thanke my stars I vnderstand my selfe a little better **now**
            [now] then in my youngger dayes when 12 giants an [houer] hower was

---

108 *hould the*] *the* added in the margin in the lt. br. ink
110 *fauour*] *a* very closely resembles an *o*
114 *heauens!*] exclamation mark added in the lt. br. ink
114-116 stage-direction and bracket added in the lt. br. ink
115 *thought*] final *t* added in the lt. br. ink
116 *see*] second *e* written over what seems to have been an *a*

120 *Royal*] *R* altered from *r*
[Fol. 4^v]
131 *Loss:*] written over *Pol*
137 *now*] added in the lt. br. ink in the margin
138 *giants*] *s* added in the lt. br. ink
138 *hower*] interlined above the deletion; both alteration and deleting strokes made with the lt. br. ink

THE FARY KNIGHT

           not enouffe for my fury I am not mad to bury all my good for
           tunes in the hungery maw of a giant. [140]

Craf: Sir y° can not refuse the fight the faits haue decreed it the gate
      to all your happines.

Loss: Pox of the fates for me I am resolued not to cope with so ter
      rible a giant as thou speaks of.

Craf: King Oberon waing wel the danger he inuits you to thought of [145]
      a way to make you surely [a onely] victorious

Los: Out with it out with it. ther are some crumbs of comfort left yet

Craf: Why he wold haue [you] me carry you to my grannams a fary wich whos
      spel will make you so impregnable that y° shall haue no difficulty to
      encounter the greatest giant euer Lancely du-lake grapplet with [150]

Loss: I thanke his grace for the care he hath on me. but dus't thinke the diuil
      and the wich thy grannã can do it?

Craf: No dificulty. Was not s^r Amides de Gall and Don Sel del Phæbo bo
      th of them inchanted and by virteu of ther spell did feats nations [t*d]
      a tiptoo to heare of.   [stod [155]

Loss: O I remember! what a blockehead am I, I an s^r Huen of Burdox
      and the blacke prince were both of them enchanted, wel get but the
      do it and I shall loue wich craft as long as I liue∼   [diuil to

                    Scæna Quinta ∼

[Fol. 5]   Enter Politico reading a letter   [160]

Los: Slid here comes Politico not a word as thou louest me of
      Oberon and fary land he will [cicumuent] circumuent me and blow vp
      my good fortunes into smoake, Machiuel was not such a politi   [all
      on as he is. he hath plots on euery part of the world, on my
      conscience Oberon is not fre frõ his conspiracyes for I heard   [165]
      him prayes fary land wch is a maine signe his mouth
      [waters] makes water after it. his spies are spread through
      the world likes Iewes or Irish men. they furnish him with

---

139 *fury*] mended or altered from another word in the dk. br. ink
139 *my good for*] y of *my* altered from dotted *i*; *for* touched up with the lt. br. ink
143 *the*] *t* heavily written over an illegible letter, perhaps an *f*
146 *surely victorious*] the writer originally wrote *sure a onely victor* and later added *ly* to *sure* in the lt. br. ink; later he deleted *a onely* and added *ious* to *victor* in the dk. br. ink
148 *Why*] *y* altered from dotted *i*
148 *me*] interlined over deleted *you*
150 *du-lake*] hyphen added in the lt. br. ink

151 *grace*] interlined above a caret
151 *me.*] period added in the lt. br. ink
151 *dus't*] apostrophe added in the dk. br. ink
154 *virteu*] *e* written over an erased *y*
154 *stod*] the deletion was made and *stod* added in the margin in the lt. br. ink
157 *both of them*] interlined above a caret in the lt. br. ink
157 *wel*] the loop of the *l* touched up with the lt. br. ink

[Fol. 5]

162 *circumuent*] interlined above the deletion, both made in the lt. br. ink

THE FARY KNIGHT

such varity of news that his estate is not sufficient to pay
for letters. he intends to build new commonwels and dstroy all [170]
the old ones. well Ile away before he spies me he'le suspect vs
vilely if he se vs to gether. where shall I fiend you 3 howers
hence to go to thy grannams.   exit Losserel:

Craf: In this very place. faile not to come and bring a present with
you for the diuil it will make the enchantment go on the better. [175]

Pol   It shall be so America is ours. the world shall stand amased to se
our triumphs. [**el] weele tread on gould whilst the richest
gemmes the red sea boast do paue the earth we make happy with our
ffame thou shall be our trumpitor and with full blasts make [presence.
the world echo our great name. Ioue send downe thy eagles [180]
send thos chariots wch to the sterry Capitol of heauen drew [th]
thee in triumph when thy powerful thunder had made thee
victor and the earth borne broud creep in to ther mothers
womb for shelter. come Ile defer my ioyes no longer Ile
erecte a pyramid made of an intire diamond in memory [185]

[Fol. 5ᵛ]   of this deade. I can not containe my selfe my breast is to ner
row for my ioyes this letter hath made me happy aboue the
rech of misery. Ile triumph for this good new, arches of stars
shall grace the solemnity. pouerty I euer banish thee the earth.
hince leaden care with thy [d*l] dul sister sorrow to hel. plea [190]
sure shall leaue the Gods and dwel with mortals Ile bring
backe the goulden age. plenty in a floud of liquid goulden
flowing frõ my Indian mines shall swime about the world

Craf: He is transported, Ile draw nerer.

Pol: What more news? from whence comes thou? [195]

Craf: ffrõ the blest Elizium happy fary-land.

Pol: ffrõ fairy. [o doth] land?

Craf   ffrõ that blest place wch to in rich nature hath impouerishd
her selfe and the world besids.

Pol   Where lise this place thou so much praseth? [200]

Craf: It is situated vnder rising Phæbus who blushes euery morning
when he climes our Hemisphere to se his light eclipsed by purer
rayes wch read eyed rubies mixed with pearle and diamons that
lie scatered one the surface of our happy ground displayes.

---

169 *varity*] the writer first wrote *vai*; then altered the *i* to *r* before proceeding
171 *he'le*] apostrophe added in the lt. br. ink
178 *the red sea boast*] interlined; in *boast* the *o*, *s*, and *t* have been mended in the lt. br. ink
179 *blasts*] final *s* added in the lt. br. ink
183 *mothers*] final *s* added in the lt. br. ink

[Fol. 5ᵛ]
188 *new*] read *news*
197 *fairy.*] the period should be a part of the deleted matter
199 *besids*] *d* written over an *s*

THE FARY KNIGHT

Pol: Pearl and diamons! this is most strange. [205]

Craf: Alas sir it is the smalest part of this blest regions prayses. the ri
uers that creepe along the flowery bosome of this blessed earth flowes nec
tor or dissolued pearle. antiquity hath wrong'd this blessed place by
telling of Hesprian gardens and ther rich fruite. tis here tis here that eue
ry tree swets vnder his goulden burthen amber and pretious gum [210]
mes porer mortals of this lower region wold bey with prouin
ces. Iasons flece was stole hence wher the porest [animal] worme
in a fur of purest gould ∼ ∼ [glitters

[Fol. 6] Pol: Monstrous! what townes are ther?

Craf Townes walled in with diamonds or with richer stones. the streats [215]
are paued with emerals and the houses cut out of pearle with spi
ring tops threaten the enameled skie.

Pol: Doth not the mighty Oberon rule ther?

Craf: In his youth he was the [happy] fortunat prince of that blest region
but growen old he fiends the purple to heauy and his trembling [220]
hand vnapt to sway the waity sceptor of so vast an empire. to
be brefe he is resolued to rule in beads of downe and leaue maiesty
in his goulden throne to be inioyed by him whos vigorous youth and
cleare eyed iudgment shall inable for so great a charge.

Pol: On my conscience good fortune I thinke courts me. I plainely see [225]
I may ioyene fary-land to my Indies. who art thou?

Craf: The man I must cease to be when my great master resignes. I am
secretary to aged Oberon imployed to fiend out happy he on whos happy
browes the faites haue decreed shall shine the rubes of the fairy diadem

Pol: And hast thou not yet found him? [230]

Craft My weary steps hath caried me through more kingdomes then euer
the glorious eye of day beheld, and yet this treasure so much sou
ght lies hid. all the sparkes of comfort wch giues motion to my
weared limbs is his name the sullen Oracle wold reueale no more.

Pol: I prethee how calst thou him? [235]

Craf: His name suets with his nature the Delphean flamen stiled him
Politico.

Pol: Heauens! this namen surpasses the musick of the spheares spea
ke it againe.

Craf: Pollitico [240]

---

205 *diamons!*] exclamation mark added in the lt. br. ink
207 *flowery*] interlined above a caret
208 *by*] added in the lt. br. ink in the margin
209 *tis here tis here*] the second *tis here* interlined above a caret
211 *porer*] first *r* heavily blotted

212 *worme*] interlined above the deletion; both made with the lt. br. ink

[Fol. 6]
228 *out*] *o* written over an illegible letter with a long upstroke like *t* or *h*
228 *whos happy*] *happy* added in the margin in the lt. br. ink

THE FARY KNIGHT

Pol: My ioyes so swel me that I must haue vent or burst. begon out
runne the winds and blesse the fairy region with this newes
Politico is found [cas] cause bels to ring
ffor now begins the triumphs of ther king.

[Fol.6ᵛ] Craf: Stay stay my soule let not this killing ioy intice the forth. O yᵉ
[celestiall powers who [245]
haue raised me to a blisse I cold scarse hope for, the richest fran
kingsense the world affords shall feede your sacred fires. but
can it be Pollitico is found?

Pol: Nay if thou turns infidel I haue done. vew me all ouer
and if thou fiends a bit as big as my nayle about me wch is not Politi [250]
co Ile forfit all my hopes in fairy land. I can not quot
the church booke for my name because it is vncertaine
where I was borne or who was my father. but you may
tel the fary lords Ile be bound to bring 7. sufficient vserers
that shall shew Pollitico in blacke and white for monyes [255]
I haue owed aboue this 12 yeares I am sure ther charity
will not let them blot it out for they are not payed yet
nor are not like til I am king of fary's.

Craf: It is a crime to delay any longer. the light shal not be mo
re swift then my payses to bring this news to fary land. [260]

Pol: Let thy returne be suddaine I long to be in my king
dome.

Craf: It shall dread leage   exit Craft

Pol: O deare fary land! Ile home and sel all I haue that I
may be able to giue a largise to my subiects at my entry. [265]
we Polletions must do so.   Exit.

Actus secundus ~

Enter Oliuer Spendals boy~

Oleu: Slid I thinke vserers dwel with the diuil they are
not to be found aboue ground. I haue bin hunting one [270]
[Fol. 7] drife foot all this morning and can not get sent of him yet I
am sure ther is not a polecat in the towne caries halfe the per

---

241 *My*] M is very doubtful and may be *m*
243 *cause*] interlined above the deletion; both made in the lt. br. ink

[Fol. 6ᵛ]
245 *soule*] interlined above a caret in the lt. br. ink
245 *O yᵉ celestiall powers*] interlined above a caret
246 *for*] interlined above the comma which follows *hope*

249 *done.*] the punctuation is doubtful but more probably a period than a comma
250 *about me*] interlined above a caret
254 *bound*] d written over an illegible letter, perhaps a *t*
258 *nor*] written over *and*
266 *Exit*] E altered from *e*

[Fol. 7]
271 *sent*] s heavily written over some illegible letter, perhaps a *y* or *g*

THE FARY KNIGHT

        fume about her that he doth. wel if I fiend him not presently
        Ile to a cunning man he wil derect me to the diuil and then I
        am sure to light on Couet for such deare friends can not liue a   [275]
        part. thes vserers are strange cattle when they are to re
        ceaue mony they anticipate the time and soner shall you
        misse the ayer then not light on them but when they are
        to pay. the Philosophers stone is not more hard to be found
        then they are. if I meet not with him presently poore Oliuer   [280]
        goes to pot. I left my master in a tauerne who measures
        my returne by his glaces if it be not speedy and with the
        monyes he sent me for he will make my crowne [*f] of Claret
        heu. I'le knock here at aduenture it lookes like a vserers
        house it is so baracadoed. (*he knocks*) liues not Mr Couet here? [285]
Ser: Sir who are you? what is your busines?
Oluer: Sure this fellow is akind to a iustice of peace he asks so many
        questions and answers none. why, I am as thou seest [on] a thing that
        crowles on 2 legs and my busines is to speake with thy master.
Ser: My master giues audience to none but thos that comes one mony   [290]
        maters and brings bags with them.
Oliuer: Nay then I am for thy master speaking with, I bring him
        bags tel him (*aside*) but they are to fill.
Ser   Sir he shall be with you imediatly.   Exit seruant
Oliuer: I doubt not. I haue sent a charme wold fech him frõ his pra   [295]
        yers if he sayed any∼

                Scæna 3^a   enter Couet

[Fol. 7^v] Couet: Sweet hart I do not know thy face but it is no matter thy
         mony will make vs acquainted. [at least sir this paper shall]
   Olue: At least sir this paper shall.   ⌈*Couet reads the letter* [300]
   Couet Thou art not affraide of spirits art thou?   ⌊*and walks*∼
   Oleu   Monstrously sir I dare not lie alone.
   Couet Nay then thou canst not helpe vs. prethe tel thy master a sad dissas
        ter keepes his mony frõ him.
   Olue: Sad indeade he will not be able to drinke sacke if it hould.   [305]
   Couet: Tel him my house is hanted. the diuil is neuer out of my coun
        ting [house] rome.

273 *if*] written over an incomplete *I*
279 *pay.*] read *pay,*
283 *of*] interlined above the deletion
284 *I'le*] apostrophe added in the lt. br. ink
287 *akind*] *a* added in the dk. br. ink
288 *a thing*] interlined above a caret and above the deletion
292 *master*] read *master's*

294 *imediatly*] *e* was first omitted and then crowded in between the *m* and *d*
294 *Exit*] *x* written over an *n*

[Fol. 7^v]
300-301 bracket added in the lt. br. ink
301 *thou?*] question mark added in the dk. br. ink and partially overlaps the bracket

THE FARY KNIGHT

Olue: Ha!
Coue: Some time he apeares in one shape some times in an other. [310]
if thou wilt thou mast go in and se him, it may be he will
vse the better then vs.
Olue: It is very vnlike I being a stranger and y° his domesticke
frinds and companions.
Couet To be plaine if thou wilt haue thy masters mony thou must
go fech it frõ the diuil. [315]
Olu: My master shall fech it him selfe or make you fech it. Ile home
and tel him so. doth he send me of a message to the diuil. exit Oluer
Coue: Thou traitor. did not I for bid you to let me speake with any
but such as brought mony?
Ser: Trew and it please your worship and had not he sayed [320]
that he brought bags, he shold haue had a positiue negatiue
answer that you were not with in~

[Fol. 8] Couet Get thee in thou rascal for thy pennance thou shalt feed on no
thing but thy selfe this 3 weaks.
Ser I beseech you sir! [325]
Coue: Prouo[g]ke not my anger verlat if it were not for wearing out
my cane I wold —
Ser: Be petiful sir.
Cou: You Rasckal — (*he stricks him*)
Ser Oh O! O! exit seruant. [330]
Cou: Now must I striue to staue of the master as I haue done
the man. Ile to my old friend Craft he'le teach me more the
art of cossening in a day then I shold lerne by my priuat stu
dy in a yeare. exit Couet.

Scæna 4ᵃ enter Snape [335]
And Shift~

Snap But did he say he wold be here presently?
Shif: Imediatly Losserello is all most mad to be enchanted he hath
bin with Craf 6 times in less then a quarter of an hower. ther is
no delaying him any longer vnlesse we spoyle all. for he can not [340]
possibly keepe it secret but will proclame it and some friend or
other will discouer him the cheate and then our marquet is spoi
led.
Snap: I apprehend thee prethee fech instantly the clothes we borowed

---

320 *Ser:*] written over *Olue* which has been partially erased
338 *enchanted*] *d* written over a *t*
341 *secret*] *t* written over a *d*
344 *borowed*] *r* written over either *tt* or *ll*

[Fol. 8]
332 *he'le*] apostrophe added in the lt. br. ink

THE FARY KNIGHT

                yester day of the players, and let vs to our worke. Ile study   [345]
                a charme the meane while — (exit shift) [I thinke I degene]
                by this light I thinke I degenerat. I was borne at Pentlow
                hill and my grannam was vile suspected for a wich and yet
                can not I make a counterfit charme. well it shall be so.

[Fol. 8ᵛ]   Shift make hast with the clothes we shall be surprized else.   [350]
      Shif: I come I come I want but your peruwig. here hast let me be
             drest first, I am the chefer person.
      Snap: Not so yᵒ sone of a tinder box I hope the wich is better then the
             diuil at any time.
      Shif: Come you are so peuish you must haue your will. giue me yʳ   [355]
             clothes. but wel remembred I must necesarily be drest first.
      Snap: Why so Shift.
      Shift: That yᵒ being the wich may haue the diuil to dresse yᵒ.
      Snap: I conceaue you be quicke.
      Shif: How doth this habit become me?   [360]
      Snap: O rarely, it is pitty thou sholdst euer weare other
      Shift: Giue me the viserd.
      Snap: ffaith thou needest none, thy face is like a visard.
      Shift: Tis no matter, it is good to be ·,· pleate. how dust like me now?
      Snap: O most vgly Belzebub can not shew a worser countinance. I dare   [365]
             be bold to say thy shape and maners will make thee passe
             for a diuil in any part of Christiandome.
      Shift   Now let vs to thee.
      Snap: Not so hasty sasboxs Ile be drest as neatly and with as much
             discretion as ere a lady wich in Lapland. runne in and fecth   [370]
             me a looking glasse.
      Shif   A looking glasse! is ther neer a frieing pan in the rome. take
             the ladle take the ladle.
      Snap: Youl do as I bid you or for all you are the diuil I'le bebold
             to beat you.   [375]
      Shif: Wel Grampogna I must obay ther is more adoe with one wich
             then 40 diuils. (Exit and *presently enters with a glasse*)
             here thou cast not se a worser face then thy one tho thou sholdst
             trauil ouer the 17 prouinces.
[Fol. 9] Shift: Dus not my hare become me?   [380]

[Fol. 8ᵛ]
  353 *Not*] *t* written over a letter now illegible, perhaps *y*; *o* perhaps written over another letter which may be an *a*
  359 *you be*] read *you. Be*
  359 *quicke*] *k* heavily written over an illegible letter
  361 *weare*] *we* written over two illegible letters which may be *at*

  363 *ffaith*] *i* inserted in the dk. br. ink
  368 *Shift*] *t* written over an *e*
  370 *ere*] initial *e* altered in the dk. br. ink from an *a*
  376 *Shif:*] written over *Snap*
  378 *cast*] read *cāst*

[Fol. 9]
  380 *Dus*] *D* written over *d*; *u* is blotted

[14]

THE FARY KNIGHT

Snap: Excellently. Medusas snaks made not a better shew then thes cur
rels. come put on you beldame ships night gowne.
Shif: How liks thow me now?
Snap: Rarely I feare the diuil will fall in loue with thee and carry thee
to hel with him and then shall I beforced to come Orpheus like with [385]
a Iews harpe and sing a pittiful song to recouer thee.
Shift: Whist, some body comes. runne or we are betraide.

Scæna 5ᵃ enter Couet and Craft~

Craft: Spirits! its a simple deuise, it may frighten children, but for
Spendal he is a gallant and to familiar with the diuil to feare [390]
Spirits.
Couet: I am vndone then vnlesse thy councel redeme me.
Craft: Well thought vpon. Spendall is a most abominable coward
go home and giue out thy house is posest with a giant. Spen
dall will conceaue it a tricke and come to yᵒ with open mouth [395]
for his mony. but before I will send yᵒ one that shall looke so dread
fully that he shall frighten him in to any conditions and not
only force him to remit the old debt but ingage him selfe
in a new to get safely of.
Couet: Most admirable counsel and better worth then the vnconscio [400]
nable fees of a layer wch I cold afford to giue thee were it
not for putting my selfe to charges. wel Ile home and put it
in execution instantly.
Craft Be spedey delay spoiles all (–Exit Couet) go ten in the
hundred deceue others and be thy selfe deceaued the time shall [405]
come when thou shalt pay me a 100 for 10 out of thos heaps

[Fol. 9ᵛ] of gould thou now sits brouding ouer and that with out interest
to. but to my busines Snap and Shift what not ready yet?

Scæna 6ᵃ

Enter Snape and Shift [410]

Snap: Almost an hower agoe. s'lid what made yᵒ bring Couet this way?
he had almost discouered vs.
Craft Tut I knew what I did. he saw you not. he is growene purblind
with counting his gould by candle light

---

381 *Medusas*] *M* written over *m*
382 *you*] read *your*
403 *instantly*] second *t* written over a *d*; *l* may
   perhaps be written over *e*
404 *spedey*] *ey* written over two illegible letters.
404 *Couet*] over *Craft*

406 *100*] the final *o* heavily mended and may
   perhaps be written over *oo*

[Fol. 9ᵛ]
413 *Craft*] dk. br. ink over *Couet*

THE FARY KNIGHT

Shif: When comes Loserello? [415]
Craft Within this halfe hower I put him of till then to speake with Politico
Snap: ffaith thy delayes will spoile all.
Craft Ile warrant y°. are the children attired like wiches?
Shif They are.
Craft And both of you knows what you are to do? [420]
Snap: I know my part if shift knowes his.
Shift: Take you no thought for me.
Craft Well then in my brace of babones and carry the busines neatly
Snap I hope you bid him bring mony with him besids the grand some we are to receaue for his enchantment. [425]
Craft He shall haue his pockets full of gould finches boyes.
Shift It shall be my prouince to take the birds.
Snap: And let it be y prouince to be trew to your companions and not deceaue vs as y° were wont.
Shift Well stinkerd you are all ways hitting me in the teeth with ould [430] deads. [done
Snap: You mungril Ile make y° giue better words.
Shift: Come one y° dog leach Ile —
Craft S'death you abominable peare of mastiue leaue of snarling and be one againe or by this light I will make you both haks [435]

[Fol. 10] meat shall my plots so wisly brought on and by my discretion ma naged be broken in the shell by a couple of todpoles.

Snap Why he.
Craft Mormoring yet Scarabe. s'lid I heare some body comeing in y° raskals and not a sillable. or. [440]

Scæna 7ª Enter Politico∼

Pol: An excelent change, and beseming a fary prince. I am no lon ger a priuat man thos durty acres that stiled me master are now turned to a more refined substance. I applaud my wit that was able to worke so rare a metamorphise as to make of land gold. it [445] will be rare at my entry to the fary crowne to make thes gold en birds in clusters sing my liberality to my subiects. bles me my genius so sone returned? what news frō fary land?

---

416 *Craft*] dk. br. ink over *Couet*
418 *Craft*] dk. br. ink over *Couet*
418 *y°.*] period added in the lt. br. ink
420 *Craft*] dk. br. ink over *Couet*
423 *Craft*] dk. br. ink over *Couet*
424 *mony*] *n* written over an illegible letter which had a tall upstroke
426 *Craft*] dk. br. ink over *Couet*
429 *vs*] *v* over illegible letter which may be an *e*

434 *Craft*] dk. br. ink over *Couet*

[Fol. 10]

439 *Craft*] dk. br. ink over *Couet*
439 *comeing*] *i* heavily written over some illegible letter; read *comeing*. In
440 *raskals*] *k* over a *c*
448 *land?*] question mark added in the lt. br. ink

THE FARY KNIGHT

Couet: My news mighty sir merited not such hast to tel it it will ma
ke your bloud curdle when you here it. [450]

Pol: What are my hopes then blasted? am I not king? for euer Phæb9
diue in to the deepe let not thy pure rayes be conscious to so bla
cke a treason. not king? with this Herculian arme Ile breake
the adamantin gates of Dis and let out night to hang the world
in morning for my losse. [not king] I am mad, I am mad. arme [455]
arme ye furies come to war against heauen, Ile be y^r captaine a
fircer charge then ere the earth borne brood gaue to Olympus
shall tel the frighted gods I am wrong'd. come come ye powers of
hel what stir ye not. nay then I se it is y^o that were the actors
of this grand mischife. Il to Ioues armary and thence fech [460]
thunder with wch Ile breake y^r strongest adamant and let
in day to fright y^r ghosts.

Cra: He is mad in deade, great sir

Pol: Screach owle besilent or my iust reuenge swifter then light

[Fol.10^v] ning shall make the meat for furies. not king? thes words [465]
include more deaths then hell cold euer boast of.

Craf Here me great prince. Polli: thy breath is infectious it is more killing
then a mandraks grone.

Craf Politico is king.

Pol: Ha what angels voice cals backe my soule frõ Radamants blacke [470]
gates? I did but dreame I hard my selfe stiled king.

Craf: The thickest [clouds] shoales of enuious clouds that striue to maske
the glorious eye of day, sols goulden rayes like poynted daggers
stob as traytors; and shall your refulgent virtues mighty prince
be eclipsd by a counterfit lustre it can not be a glow worme [475]
shold out shine the sune or so poore a thing as Losserello vey
with great Politico.

Pol: Ha! Losarello? by my great hopes Ile cut him in to atoms and
scater them before the northeren winds. Losarello betwene me
and the fary diadem? by heauens [Ilp] Ile pull pale death from [480]
out his iron den and hurle him at the monster.

Craf: Sir let y^r passions cole they darken the bright flame of reason
wch must light y^o to y^r reuenge~

Pol: My wrongs my wrongs will do it. shold he hide himselfe wher
the earth hids all her riches my wrongs wold light me to him [485]

---

449 *Couet:*] read *Craft:*
454 *Dis*] D perhaps altered from *d*
455 *arme*] *r* heavily mended
456 *arme*] *r* heavily mended
457 *brood*] second *o* perhaps altered from an *a*
460 *and*] *d* is heavily mended; it appears that a *d* was written over the upper loop of an *f* and then later touched up for clarity

463 *Cra:*] *ra* over two letters which appear to be *ou*

[Fol. 10^v]

467 *Here*] *r* heavily mended, perhaps deleting an *a*
467 *Polli:*] interlined above a caret
485 *wold*] altered from *will*

THE FARY KNIGHT

                and my iust angre powerful as Ioues thunder strike him deade.
Craf: Let not y^r forward valiour throw away a life so pretious to the
        gods as yours. the verlot knowing whõ he wrong'd and fering
        y^r iust vengance shold meet his crime neuer walks but guar
        ded with a band of souldiers deare incounter armies.   [490]
Pol: Did furies guarde him, or were he hegged with lightning I
        wold through and kill him.
Craft   Your courage mighty sirs speakes you more then man and [wis
        dome wiser then Apollo] only worthy that great dignity the

[Fol. 11]   faites haue decreed your but let not your valiour open   [495]
        a passage [to] for your enemies to reach that life all the Gods seake
        to preserue and wch once gone the world must needs deplore
        it with a vniuersal sorrow. let wisdome stere y^r actions and [let]
        mortals know y^r prudence is as great as your corage wch to
        your enemies portends more ill then 1000 flameing comits   [500]
        might I be worthy to dictate to your thoughts I cold suggest a
        secure and reddy way to y^r iust vengance~
Pol: Secure and ready speake it and thou shalt be my better gene9
        the greatest honours the fary court can giue shal be conferd vpon
        thee I will make the vice Roy vnder me.   [505]
Craf: Thus then sir may y^o expiate y^r wronges with the traitours
        life. some streats of liues one Couet a vserer whos gould ha
        th caused all your truble for here he raysed large summes
        with wich he bribed y^r fairy peares to take him for ther prin
        ce. hether some 6 [day]s hower hence [will] he'l come for fresh   [510]
        and here may you take y^r iust reuenge of him my letter shall [supplies
        gaine y^o entrance to the vserer.
Pol: Alas it is to long to defer the pleasures of a kingdome.
Craf   It is not necesary to put of y^r coronation. it will be princely after
        y^o are crowned to procede to iustice and execute the traitor   [515]
Pol: fflie backe with wings of hast and tel my subiects I attend ther
        comeing to tender ther allegiance they owe ther prince.
Craf: I go sir but wher shall I fiend y^r grace at my returne with
        the fary lords?
Pol: At my house, my palace I shold say I must accostome my selfe [520]
        to more kingly termes
Craf: The gods preserue your maiesty.

[Fol. 11]

495 *your but*] read *yours, but*
495 *valiour*] *i* has been squeezed in later
496 *for*] interlined above the deletion
505 *vice*] *ic* written heavily over two illegible letters
508 *here*] *r* heavily mended

510 *hower*] interlined above the deletion; the undeleted *s* of *days* is presumably to be attached to *hower*
510 *he'l*] apostrophe and *l* were inserted in the dk. br. ink
522 *Craf:*] written a half-line above its proper place, and for clarity joined to *The* with an oblique pen stroke

THE FARY KNIGHT

Pol: This it is to be confident I derst neuer fight in my whole life
[Fol.11ᵛ] yet by making this shew of valior knowing my enemy to be a wor
ser cowerd then my selfe I shall haue my name in rowled amung [525]
the worthyes of faryland. wel Ile home and set my house in order
to receaue the fary lords~

Actus Tertius ~

Scena 1ᵃ *enter* Craf *and* Losserello~

Craf Slid wher haue you bin all this while? the diuil hath expected [530]
yᵒ this 2 howers. I had much ado to hold him he was going away
in a snuffe.
Los: I hope he is not gone.
Craf: No it cost me some thing to stay him.
Los: What didst giue him? [535]
Craf: By this light he was in such a collor at yʳ stay I was forced to send for
a whole butte of wine to coolee him. it was for your sake I hope
youl pay for it:
Loss: Pay for it? Ile pay for it twise ouer. thou shalt get as much by me
as my hostes. but prethee tel me doth the diuil loue wine? [540]
Craft Monstrously! what do yᵒ thinke makes so many vintners breake in the
City but his vngodly gut that feches of whole hogsheads at a draught?
Losse: Nay I like him neer the worse because he is a good fellow~
Craft: Good fellow! why ther is neuer a frolicke or ioyuiall meeting in the
[towne but he is the
cheife at it. the ranters were tought that noble quality of [545]
and swearing by him. [drinking
Loss: Thou telst me wounders I hope I shall creepe in to his company af
ter my enchantment.
Craft: Thou shalt lad Ile bring the acquainted with him. I am no small man
[Fol. 12] in his fauour my brother is cheife butler of his wine seller if thy [550]
occasions cal thee to hell I doubt not but for my sake thou shalt be diue
lishly entertained and damable welcome.~
Loss: I shall thinke of imbracing this courtisie when I am old and weary
of king Oberons court for I am resolued to spend the last part of my life
in drinking. but now let vs to our busines for if we delay the diuil [555]

---

523 *confident*] *t* crowded in after the next word was written

[Fol. 11ᵛ]

527 *the*] *e* written heavily over *es*; supply *exeunt*
537 *butte*] originally written *bute*; the second *t* was crowded in later in the dk. br. ink and the original final *e* touched up in that ink

541 *thinke*] *t* written over an illegible letter, perhaps a *c*
542 *draught?*] over *drauft*
544 *or ioyuiall meeting*] interlined above a caret

[Fol. 12]

553 *thinke*] *k* over an illegible letter, perhaps a *g*

THE FARY KNIGHT

                to long he will haue the other tuch at it and what a score then shall
I haue to wipe of?
Craf   I will call him and my grannam to dispach y° preasently.
Loss   But stay dids not tell me the diuil drunke a whole butte?
Craf: Mary did he. do y° thinke I wold cossen y°?   [560]
Loss: No, no. but dost thinke the diuil is yet sober? if he shold enchant me
in his drinke and it proue voide I were in a fine picle.
Craft: Best of all when he is drunke. what he dus then is most efficatious.
Loss: Nay then he shall haue the other cup here are 5 peeces bid him
drinke this for my sake.   [565]
Craft: I go I go.   exit Craf
Loss: When I am enchanted. I am resolued to fall in league with all the
ballatmakers in the towne. they shall writ my aduentures. it will get
them more mony I am confident, then the famous history of Tom thu
mbe, Gie of Woricke or Beuis of South hampton for I am resolued   [570]
to fight with none but Giants and thos of the largest sise. but here
comes Craft and his grannā~

                Scæna 2ᵃ enter Craft and the Wich

Craf: Here she is.
Loss: What that old hagge.   [575]
Craf: Peace, peace she hath ride coomites with thin halfe hower on
a distafe for your sake salute her I say.
Loss: Thou woldst not haue me kisse the diuil
Craft: Better language she approches downe one your knees and [wri*]
[Fol.12ᵛ]   anske her blessing while I present [her to] y° to her.   [580]
Loss: But wher is the Diuil must I not haue his blessing to?
Craf   He will come by and by he is with in a drinking, now downe one yʳ
knees and wriggle she hath a stately presence Ile speake for y°: most lerned
maddam of the laplanders this gentleman my pretious friend pricked
forward with a noble desier of geting honour in king Oberons court   [585]
implores yʳ powerful spels to make him inuincible it is a fauour I con
fesse and great one wch he askes. but if yʳ beldameship please to grant
it y° shall fiend him as deutiful and and as ready to serue y° as any
diuil you haue.

559 *butte?*] written in the dk. br. ink over *but?*;
    a second *t* is written over the original final
    e, an *e* over the original question mark, and
    a new question mark appended
563 *most*] o heavily mended, perhaps over some
    illegible letter
564 *shall*] s over an *h*
566 *I go I go*] second *I* over a *g*
570 *mbe*] e over an *s*

570 *Gie*] *ie* altered from *u*
572 *comes*] s crowded in after the next word had
    been written
573 *2*] heavily mended, perhaps over a *3*
576 *halfe*] *h* mended, perhaps over some illegible
    letter

[Fol. 12ᵛ]
    587 *askes*] *kes* heavily mended

[20]

THE FARY KNIGHT

Loss: Thou woldst not haue me wait vpon the wich woldst thou? [590]
Craf: Peace, heare what my grannam sayes.
Wich I feare he is not capable of incantation. hath he any thing transi
tory about him?
Craf: Maddam he shall be serched.
Loss: Who shall search me? [595]
Craf: Why who shold? the diuil man, dus't not know that?
Loss: Prethee aske thy grannã whether thou mayst not. I am very
looth to haue the diuil so neer about me he smels so strong of
brimstone.
Craf: Ile trie what I can do. y° must not be so nice when y° come [600]
about thes businesses. maddam the gentleman desiers y°l dispen
ce with his being searched by the diuil.
Wich: It can not be granted our spel will not fasten on him as long
as he keepes a crosse of coyne about him.
Craf: With y^r beldomeships leaue maddam to do my friend a curte [605]
sie Ile purifie him frõ all the drosse that may checke y^r great
worke and hinder his incantation.
Wich: Well do it but if y° haue not all we shall be trubled to haue
[Fol. 13] the diuil search him ouer againe.
Craf: I hope ther will be no need. his discretion will not let him concea [610]
le any thing. Loss: no by this light will I not.
Craf: It is not y^r best way if y° intend to inrowle y^r name amoung
the worthys of fayryland do not conceale a penny. wher lies
your mony?
Loss: In my fob. [615]
Craft Is heere all?
Loss: I euery penny.
Craf: I will giue it my grannã to dispose of. maddam the gentle
man sends y° this to bestow in charity vpon poore hobgob
lings. [620]
Wich: Child call in Mistophiles y^r friend is false here is not all.
Craf: Now are you in a fine picle the diuil must come and
search you?
Loss: Deare Craft speake for me to thy grannã as I am a gentle
man I haue not more then a crowne in gould my M^rs [625]
gaue.

---

590 *woldst thou*] originally written *wold thou*; the *st* was crowded in in the lt. br. ink and then the *t* of *them* was mended in the same ink
592 *Wich*] written over *Loss:*
592 *thing*] g written over a t
596 *dus't*] apostrophe added in the lt. br. ink
601 *y°l*] the writer wrote *y°* and then formed the t of what was probably going to be *to* before he changed his mind and altered the *t* to *l*
607 *his*] written over *our*

[Fol. 13]
611 *Loss:*] interlined
616 *heere*] second *e* altered from an *a*
625 *a*] interlined above a caret

THE FARY KNIGHT

Craft   And wold y^o vndo your selfe for a trifle? cast it away presen
tly I had rather you shold haue throne 20 crownes away
then haue concealed it. Ile make [yo] an appolagy for you
to my Grannã. so y^o haue nomore. as y^o loue y^r selfe confesse   [630]
for when the diuil comes he will smell it, and then he will
so pinch y^o y^{r}our body will not be in case this 6 weaks. besids
if y^o conceale any thing the charme will be of no force
and then if y^o haue y^r braines beaten out with a giants
club thanke y^r selfe.   [635]

Losso: No Craft as I hope to be a knight of fary-land I haue not
any thing in the shape of mony.

[Fol.13^v] Craf: Maddam my friend implores y^r beldameships pardon for
a falte not couitousnes but loue made him cõmit the mo
ny beig his mistres fauour he sought to preserue.   [640]

Wich   We pardon him bid him draw neer that we may stroake
him and then begin the Orgies.

Craf: Go to her y^o heare what she sayes.

Loss: I but of what size are her nayeles? I feare she will claw
me now for thinking to cossen her.   [645]

Craft: Be of good courage my grannã is a gentle creature

Wich: Come child of perdition.

Loss: Oh ho ho!

A Charme 1

Wich   Thus thus I do begin   [650]
To put the on an other skin
Which shall sword and speare repel.
Come ye spirits that do dwel
In the deepes of Acherone
Bring me Cerberus his fome.   [655]
Come ye watery spirits all
Be ye present at our call
Bring with y^o vnto the spell
The sacred iuce of Lethe's well.
Bring the poison of Æchidne   [660]
Wee'l make him sone as mad as we be.

---

629 *for*] *r* interlined above a caret
632 *y^o y^{r}our*] the writer first wrote *y^r body*; he then, or later, altered the *r* of *y^r* to an *o*, making the word *y^o*, and interlined *y^r* over a caret; still later he touched up the *y* of the interlineation and added *our*, both in the lt. br. ink, forgetting to delete the *r*
636 *Losso*] over *Craf*

637 *thing*] *g* over what seems to have been a *k*

[Fol. 13^v]
639 *cõmit*] *i* altered from an *e*
640 *beig*] read *bei̇g*
641 *stroake*] *a* written over a *k*
644 *nayeles?*] question mark crowded in later
653 *Come*] written over an erasure

THE FARY KNIGHT

Loss: Maddam deare maddam I beseech you heare me
Wich: Peace varlet.
[Fol.14] Loss: I am not acquainted with the constitution of euery di
uil wherefore I beseech y^r beldameship to make as few as [665]
possibly y^o can acquainted with my enchantment. Speake for
me Craft. Craf: y^o may be suer she will do it the best way she can

Charme 2.

Wich
    Come ye gobblings that do creepe
    Throught dores when the maids are aslepe, [670]
    Bring the entrels of the rat
    With the mewings of the cat.
    Ye nimble ffaunes and siluans all
    Be not absent at our call
    Gether hemlocke at mid night, [675]
    When as Cynthia shineth bright.
    Gather night shade Hellebore
    With the Mandraks grones vptore,
    Bring me molds eyes adders tungs
    Bring the crokeing toads lungs. [680]
    Come ye spirits of the ayer
    To our charmes make swift repare.
    Bring me poyson frõ the moone
    And be present with vs soone.

Los: Craft prethe aske thy grannam what must be done [685]
[Fol.14^v] [*it] with all this she calls for if it be to be eaten she shold ha
ue giuen me notice of it beforehand that I might haue pre
pared my stomack here is as much as wil keepe me chowing
this sennight.

Wich   Wher is my brasen knife Ile wound my arme [690]
    And as it bleeds Ile speake a charme
    Shall make the faries rise from depest hell
    And force thes sliggish spirits to our spell

[Fol. 14]
667 *Craf:*] interlined above a caret
670 *dores*] the reading is somewhat uncertain; the *o* is very close to an *a*
672 *mewings*] *s* added in the lt. br. ink
675 *mid*] *d* heavily written over two letters, the first of which seems to be a *g* or a *y* and the second perhaps an *n*

679 *molds*] the reading is somewhat uncertain; the *l* is very heavily mended, perhaps over some illegible letter, and there is a dot, which is probably accidental, over the second minim of the *m*
685 *Craft*] *r* is written over what seems to be an *h*; there is then a blot deleting some illegible letter before the *a* follows

[23]

THE FARY KNIGHT

Charme 3

   ffrom stygian deepes black night arise   [695]
   And spread thy sables ouer the spangled skies.
   Hells power is contemned ye armed furies come
   And ioyne with me in Chaos for to turne
   Earth ayre and heauen. nay quicke or I wil send
   Through earths darke bosome murmurs that shall rend [700]
   In peeces the blacke gates of Dis and lay
   Auernus open to aproching day.

Los: Now am I in a fine picle I wish I had bin fairely hang'd
   when first I thought of being inchanted she hath calld for
   the furies and when they come for certaine they will eat [705]
   me. Craft wher art thou?
Craf: Here
Los: Art thou not affraide?
Craf: No no be of good courage.
[Fol.15] Los: what doth thy grannã do?   [710]
Craf She is houlding conference with the diuil
Wich Nor yet

   [Nay then Ile set the elements at wars
   Midnight shall se the day and n* st**]
   Nay then Ile make the elements to fight
   Midnight Ile turne to day midday to night.
   Ile murmur out a charme shall make the mone   [715]
   Poyson'd efrighted frõ out her siluer chariot come.

    Triphon Cocabel Camas

   Nor yet my rage begins to swell
   Darkenes diuils night and hell
   I charge ye streight obay my spell.   [720]
   O dus it take the? the earth begins to tremble the spir
   its are in ther rise bring me fresh veruine to bind my
   head.

Los: Alas Craft what wil become of me?
Craf: Expect with patiance and admiration the euent   [725]

[Fol. 14ᵛ]
 695 *deepes*] third *e* written over an *s* and the final *s* appended before the next word was written
 698 *in*] interlined above a caret
 700 *earths*] *s* added in the dk. br. ink
 704 *calld*] *d* is imperfect, but the spelling was probably intended for *calld* rather than *cald*

[Fol. 15]
 715 *a*] written over what seems to be the erased beginning of an *I*

716 *efrighted*] interlined above *Poyson'd* and the writer then forgot to delete one or the other; in *Poyson'd* the *P* is heavily mended, perhaps over a *p*, and the *s* is mended perhaps over some illegible letter; the reading of *efrighted* is somewhat uncertain since the initial *e* merges in the ornamental stroke of the *P* and the word may be *frighted*
725 *admiration*] *ad* interlined above a caret

[24]

THE FARY KNIGHT

Loss: I wold giue my legs and armes to come well of.
Wich Keepe kepe your circle if frō thence you stray
To blacke Auernus presently away
ffuries in snake bands will drag your soule
Where it with flames tortur'd for ere shall howle [730]
Los: I beseech your beldomeship may not Craft be in the cir
cle with me I dare not be alone.
[Fol.15ᵛ] Craf: Why I shall be enchanted to.
Los: What then? I hope your betters are enchanted.
Craf: Why then the diuil must haue duble pay and by my faith [735]
I can not go to the cost of it.
Los: I will sel the rest of my land but thou shalt be enchan
ted to, I am resolued to make the my lance prosade
when I am dubd Sʳ Losserello del fumo by Oberon.
Craf: On thes condition I come to [thee] you. [740]

The Diuil rises out of the ground

W[**]h: How dearest thou thus delay my powerfull charme?
Did not the accents of my voice alarme[?]
Hell and the furies? didst not quake to heare
The horrid murmurs that my words did bare? [745]
Diu: I did and to the deepes made swift repaire
To fech thes simples wich frō thence I bare.
Wich What hast thou brought?
Diu: In this viol mixed be
The strongest poysons of Tartare. [750]
Here is Achonit ouergrone,
Here is Cerberus his fome,
Here is Alecto's milke Tisiphonies haire
Mixed with the vipers bloud she doth ware.
Here is an adder Megæra did breed [755]
With the dire poison wheron she doth feed.
Here is sacred Lethes iuce [which]
Which in charmes you wont to vse.

---

727 *kepe*] *k* heavily mended, perhaps over some illegible letter
727 *you*] interlined above a caret
731 *Craft*] *C* altered from *c*

[Fol. 15ᵛ]
742 *W[**]h:*] a large accidental blot has made illegible two letters which are probably *ic*
743 *alarme*] the question mark following was erased

747 *bare*] *ar* over *ea*
749 *Diu:*] over an erasure
754 *ware*] *r* mended to delete an *i* following the *a*
755 *Here*] *r* heavily mended to delete either an *a* or an *e* after the first *e*
755 *breed*] second *e* altered from an *a*
757 [*which*]] erased
758 *Which*] heavily written over an illegible erasure

THE FARY KNIGHT

[Fol.16] Wich:1 Wel done my fine for this thou then shalt sucke
My bloud vntil my vaines be quiet dried vp. x [760]

Enter the 2 Wich

Speake hag wher hast thou bin?
What hast thou done what dost thou bring? [770]
Wich 2   I haue bin gathering Cyprus bows
ffig tre leaues and poppy that grows
In yonder churchyard wher I haue
Killed a sextone making a graue.

Enter the 3 Wich   [775]

Wich 1 Wher were you?   I charge you tell
Why y° did delay my spell?
Wich 3   I heard you charme and I went to call
The snaks bread vnder younder wall.
I spoake a spel and out they came   [780]
And here is ther bloud with the toads braine.
Wich 1 Well done my hag for this thou then shalt be
In our great art the [second] chefest next to me.

Enter a 4 Wich

An other late.   what caused this delay   [785]
Thou meager hag I charge the streight to say
Wich 4   I haue bin gathering wolues haires
The mad dogs fome and adders eares
A mandrake out of the earth I haue tore
Here is all this what wold you haue more. [790]

*But first backe to the stygian shades repaire
And fech for Craf the maiecke lute left there
By Orphious when for his Eridice [he]
He was a suppliant to great Hecate*

x

Craf: peace [765] *the diuil brings the lute.* Los: why sarrah are you so vnmanerly as not to make a hand and kisse y[r] lege to the diuil~

Los: harke Craft [thy] preferment is coming to the thou must be arch fidlar to the diuil.

[Fol. 16]
759 *fine*] the first minim of the *n* deletes what seems to be the start of an *e*, as if the writer had first thought of writing *fiend*
761 *stygian*] *a* heavily written over another letter, perhaps an *e*
762 *fech*] *h* heavily mended over an illegible letter
763 *Eridice*] *E* heavily mended over an illegible letter, perhaps an *e*
764 *Hecate*] a large accidental blot partially obscures *ate*
769 *Speake*] written over an illegible erasure
769 *bin?*] question mark added in the lt. br. ink
770 *bring?*] question mark added in the lt. br. ink
772 *poppy*] *o* written over a *p*
776 *Wher were*] originally written *when ere*; some mendings in the dk. br. ink are seemingly intended as a correction to the present reading

777 *spell?*] an original period is altered to a question mark in the lt. br. ink
781 *the*] interlined above a caret
783 *chefest*] interlined above the deletion

THE FARY KNIGHT

[Fol.16ᵛ] Wich 1   ffor thy reward I put the on
                This veruin garland of my one.
                              Enter an other Wich 5
                Come meager hag tel what hath wrought
                This this thy delay what hast thou brought.   [795]
     Wich 5   I haue brought you childrens fat
                The dead mens bones which you did lacke
                [A mandrake out of the earth I haue
                Tore here is all this what wold you haue more]
                Here is the bassilisks bloud and the vipers skin
                And now your Orgies you may begin.
     Wich 1   Come hags and furies hedge me round   [800]
                Whilst the maiecke timberils sound
                Performe iust rites to Hecate
                To the ground each bend a knee
     Los: Craft must not we kneel to?
     Craf   No no!   [805]
     Loss: Why yᵒ raskall wil you not do as your better do before you?
               Do not you se the diuil knele and the wich your grannã?
     Wich 1   So so my hags thes rites are wel pformed
                ffor all our simples are to serpents turned
                Rise then and dance a maieck round   [810]
                About me whilst I bury in the ground.
                Our mixed poysons which shall infuse a spirit
                In to this lad shall make him sone inherit
                The fary region and cast downe [giants]
                Giants whos wait will shake the ground.   [815]
[Fol.17] Los: Harke Craft she says I must inherit fariland and kill giants
                to.
     Craf   Why so yᵒ must Ile warrant you. do yᵒ thinke my grannam
               and the diuil takes all this paynes for nothing?
     Los: O it will be rare the boyes will adore me when they heare I   [820]
               am enchanted and how I kill giants.
                         Here is to be exhibited an anticke
                               Dance of wiches~

[Fol. 16ᵛ]
796 *childrens*] *c* over some illegible letter, perhaps the start of a *d*
798 *bassilisks*] *k* over some illegible letter, perhaps an *x*
800 *hedge*] originally *hege*; the *d* was written over the original *g*, the *g* over the original *e*, and final *e* added, all before the next word was written
801 *sound*] *d* altered from a *t*

806 *raskall*] *k* apparently written over some illegible letter, perhaps a *c*
806 *better*] read *betters*
814 [*giants*]] erased

[Fol. 17]
818 *my*] *m* over some letter which had a long upstroke
821 *kill*] *k* over a *c*
822 *be*] interlined above a caret

THE FARY KNIGHT

Wich 1 Enuffe my hags now each dispence
    Vpon this lad her influence. [825]
    Rub him ouer that he neer feele
    The poynt or edge of biting steele.
    Take him by the nose and pul it
Los: Oh, oh, O!
Wich 1 He is now fre frõ sword and bullet. [830]
    Our charme is done now each hag go   exeunt veneficæ
    Quickly home for the Cocke doth crow   Omnes præter jam
Loss: Craft am I sufficiently enchanted thinks thou?
Craf Thou art my Roseclero thanke my grannam for it
Los: O Craft for this fauour I loue her more tenderly then euer [835]
    the diuil did.
Craf: You se she hath taken extraordnary paynes she must
    be considered.
Los: She shall thou diuils darling what shal I giue her?
Craf: Ene what you will, you haue fary-land enoufe faith [840]
    giue her thos durty akers you haue here they will ser
    ue her to dance the hey in with her wiches by moone
    light.
[Fol.17ᵛ] Los: She shall haue it my rascal and I will haue thee to be my
    Lance Prosade to carry my sword [be] and sheld before me thro [845]
    ugh the bloudy feilds of Mars.
Craf: Here comes my grannam downe one your knees and
    thanke her.
Los: Honoured lady of Laplanders I your newly valiant seruant
    thanke you and in token of gratitude vows to weare [850]
    your beldamships picture painted on my sheild it will ma
    ke me passe for a knight of the maiden head how liks thou
    the deuice Craft
Craf Rarely it will looke so like Medusas countinance it wil be
    taken for your mistres picture. [855]
    Wich 1 My valiant boy I do impart
        Such courage to thee shall make start
        The stoutest Giants and thee bring
        To be of faires crowned king.   Exit Wich
Los: Thanks gratious maddam. [860]
Craf: Kisse her departing part.
Los: Is she gon?

---

832 *jam*] read *ũam*

[Fol. 17ᵛ]

850 *gratitude*] second *t* over a *d*; the first minim of the *u* may perhaps delete the start of an *e*

850 *vows*] *s* probably squeezed in later

852 *me*] interlined above a caret

854 *Rarely*] *ly* interlined above a caret

THE FARY KNIGHT

Craf: I, Ile warrant you a 1000 miles by this
Los: Now raskal let vs to the giant I haue a monstrous mind
      to trie the toughnes of my new constitution. [865]
Craf: Tis to sone yet go home and let the charme settle vpon
      you 2 or 3 howers and then to the combat.
Los: Marry and thou sayest right it shall be so
                            exeunt.

[Fol. 18]   *Actus Quartus* [870]

          Scæna prima~

Enter Spendall with tapsters armed with
clubs. the vintners boy carrying the colours a quart
pot on the top of a pole. each instead of a belt ha
uing a hoope crosse him with a pot tied to it. in this [875]
equipage a barrel beaten before them for a drumb,
one with a tobaccho pipe for a fluite playing by the
durummer they march 2 or 3 times about the stage.

Spen: Stand 1 stand 4 stand.
Spen: Corporal? [880]
4   Corporal?
Corp By and by anan anan sir.
5   Troope vp to our captaine.
Corp I must prime first.
      Now noble captaine what is your will? [885]
Spend: Bare the word of command to our soldiers, bid them stand
      in ther roes and charge. tel them we are bent on seruice.
Corp: Gentleman and souldiers you hear what our captaine sayes.
All all We do we do
6   Helpe me to pul out my gun sticke. [890]
7   Hould my picke tel I prime.
Spen Are all ready?
All: All all.
[Fol.18ᵛ]Spen: Take the worde of command giue fire. *(they all drink)*
      done like valiant sones of Mars and Bacchus. sirrah put [895]
      downe the drume for me to sit on whilst I speake to my
      souldiers.

---

864 *raskal*] *k* over a *c*
[Fol. 18]
  875 *it.*] interlined above a caret
  877 *playing*] *pl* heavily mended, perhaps over illegible letters
  878 *durummer*] first *r* heavily mended, perhaps over an illegible letter

878 3 *about*] 3 over a letter which may be a *t*; the *a* of *about* seems altered from some letter which may be an undotted *i*
878 *times*] interlined
879 *Spen:*] perhaps written over the figure *1*
879 1] over 2
879 4] over 3

THE FARY KNIGHT

                Gentlemen and fellowes in armes I can not doubt your vali
                our whos inuincible crownes I know to haue bin battered
                with pots of all sizes and yet not subdued, whõ I know   [900]
                to haue demanded a reckning of the roaring boies
                when [Mars] Bacchus hath triumphed in ther blouds and dared to
                call Mars cowerd.   I can not I say doubt your corage
                being so well acquainted with your passiue fortitude how
                you haue bin cudgled by all nations and all most all re   [905]
                ligions knowing how your valiant hinder parts ha
                ue defied the feete of all liuing and incounterd more
                toes then ther are knaues in the kingdome, but to shew
                the weaknes of the foe we are to deale with all and the
                rich garland wch will crowne the victorie my va   [910]
                liant Hectors I addresse my selfe to you.   thus far vn
                der my bloudy stander haue you marched vncontrow
                led.   the castle we are to lay seage to is in sight wher
                all the resistance like to me your approued valuor
                is what Couet and his cat can make.   I doubt not but now   [915]
                Mars is dancing a caranto in your bloud and you are
                all ready scaling the wals distroying this vserer this ene
                my to your sacred profession.   fall on my Marmidons.

[Fol. 19]   Confound this rat of Nilus, this monster.   but why do?   I say mon
                ster?   this diuil this sacrelegious diuil that hath imprisoned   [920]
                infinit goulden angels in his mouldy coffers.   harke they im
                plore your valiant hands to set them at liberty.   and for
                reward promise themselues yours.
        Draw 1 By this light and we will do it
        Draw 2 March forward captaine   [925]
        Spen: Spoake like sones of Mars take vp the drume boy and beate
                a dreadfull march before vs.

                           Scæna 2ª ∼

                        Enter Craft∼

        Craf   Helpe helpe or we are all distray'd.   [930]
        Spend What is the matter?

[Fol. 18ᵛ]
  900 *sizes*] *z* over an *s*
  902 *Bacchus*] interlined above the deletion
  908 *are*] *a* over some illegible letter with a long
      upstroke
  914 *me*] read *meet*

[Fol. 19]
  919 *monster.*] period is well below the line and
      rather doubtful
  919 *do?*] question mark was apparently crowded
      in later; read *do*
  929 *Craft*] *f* heavily mended, perhaps over a *t*
  931 *Spend*] dk. br. ink over *Loss:*

THE FARY KNIGHT

Craft	Sir rally vp your valiant followers and for the publick	
	safty attempt the encounter of a Giant who hath within	
	this quarter of an hower distrayed 3000 citizens. his iron club	
	neer fals but it sends more to the Stygian lac[e]ke then	[935]
	Charon can ferry ouer at once.	
Spend	Wher, wher is?	
Craf:	He liues at a vserers cald Couet and now is distraying the	
	peple 2 streats of. harke do y° not heare the cryes of [d*ing]	
	deying men	[940]
1	Marry do I	
2	And I to.	
3	And I Roger as playne as if I were by them.	
Craf:	What will not feare doe?	
[Fol.19ᵛ] 4	Captaine y° know it was not in our articles when we listed	[945]
	our selues vnder y° to kil giants.	
Spen:	It was not nether do I intend it. my valiant friends retire,	
	I count him most coragious that hids him selfe securest.	
All	Weel do our best then to proue our selues valiant.	
1	Stay Peter take me along with you I can not runne	[950]
	so fast.	
Craf	What power hath feare ouer base minds. I haue dis	
	pached thes now must I to my fary lords. Snap and shift	
	what not ready yet?	
Snap	All are ready besids vs and we haue but newly put of our	[955]
	couniuring habit.	
Craf	Ye haue tought the children how to behaue themselues?	
	can they do the dance?	
Snap	Excellently.	
Craf	And they haue ther song behart?	[960]
Shif	At ther fingers ends.	
Craf	Good. by this light I heare somebody comeing for certaine it	
	Politico. in and be ready presently. I appointed him to be hea	
	re iust at this time.	

932 *vp*] *p* mended over an illegible letter
934 *citizens*] the reading is uncertain; the *e* has perhaps been altered from an *o*
935 *sends*] originally *sens*; the *d* was written in the dk. br. ink over the original final *s* and a new final *s* added in that ink
935 *lac[e]ke*] *la* and *ke* are clear; the central part of the word has been mended and it appears that the medial *e* was deleted and the *c* touched up
936 *Charon*] *h* over some letter, probably an *a*
937 *Spend*] dk. br. ink over *Los:*

943 *if*] over *I*

[Fol. 19ᵛ]

947 *I*] over an illegible letter
950 *Peter take*] *P* of *Peter* altered from *p*; *ta* of *take* written over two illegible letters
955 *are*] over a three-letter word, the last letter of which was an *s*
957 *themselues*] *u* over an erased *f*
963 *Politico*] a large accidental blot partially obscures the *P* and could just possibly hide a preceding word *is*

THE FARY KNIGHT

        Scæna 3ᵃ   enter Politico   [965]
        In a ffaire-habit~

Craf: The Gods preserue our mighty prince Politico
Pol: How liks thou me now shall I not be more pleasing to my
         subiects thus attired then in the weads of Mortality?
Craf: You wil dread leage. for trust me euenso withsuch a   [970]
         gracefull maiesty and so attired was ancient Oberon when
         by the voice of all the fairy lords he was chose king of our vast
         empire.
[Fol.20] Pol: When wil my [farg] fary peares arriue?
Craf: They attend yʳ grace expecting when they may be admitted   [975]
         to yʳ presence to performe ther allegiance.
Pol: Bid them enter.
Cra: Shift are you ready
Shif   Yes yes is it time to come in?
Craf: I I presently.   [980]

        Scæna 4ᵃ the musicke sounding enter
        One bearing the Eutacusticon. another a
        wodden sword. the 3 a sceptor the 4 an
           old cloake for a purple~

ffar 1   Illustrious prince tho your [ef] refulgent virtues giues yᵒ   [985]
         iust title to the worlds empire tho yʳ valior whch speaks you
         more then Mars and prudence wiser then [App] Apollo
         haue with their refulgent rayes dazeld the eyes of kings
         and forced them to lay ther crownes and sceptours at yʳ feet
         wch not with standing yʳ greatnes hath spurn'd at as not   [990]
         worthy the touch of yʳ Royall hand.
Pol: Trew Presbiter Ihon hath courted me I know not how
         oft to ease him of his purple and sway his goulden sceptour
         telling me the rubies of his deadem wold haue a far bright
         er lustre on my fore head then one his. tis well knowen the   [995]
         great Turke hath often proferd to become Christian on con

---

967 *Gods*] *s* added in the lt. br. ink
970 *trust*] the writer started to form an *e* after the final *t* but stopped before completing the letter

[Fol. 20]
974 [*farg*]] the deletion probably made because a false stroke caused the final *y* to resemble a *g*

982 *another*] the writer first wrote *and*, then changed the *d* to an *o* before proceeding with the *ther*
985 *virtues*] *u* over an erased *y*
987 *prudence*] first *e* apparently altered from an *a*
992 *Presbiter*] *b* over an *s*
994 *telling*] *t* altered from some letter, perhaps a *T*

THE FARY KNIGHT

     dition I wold weare his his turbat, yet I cold not fiend in my hart
     to imbrace it knowing the Turkish empyre far to little for
     my greatnes I shold not haue rome to expatiat in
ffar 2 Not with standing thes great profers mighty Sir daine to   [1000]
     weare this fairy diadem wch tho it now appeares ruffe and
[Fol.20ᵛ] hairy to yʳ sight inured to mortal obiects will when you haue
     shaked of yʳ mortality discouer more radiant light then
     the spangl'd firmament when left by the lampe of day and
     piect forth such pure rayes as shall confirme mortals not Phæ [1005]
     bus but yᵒ inlighten them. it is lin'd with fortunes apron and
     therfore ought to sit but on his head who is her darling and
     and the worlds glory.
ffar: 3 Take great prince this sword made by the destinies wher
     in are wrought the faits of mortals, beleue not yʳ eyes   [1010]
     wch tels yᵒ it is wood when once yᵒ are parg'd frõ the dregs
     of mortality you shall se it brighter then lighting display
     flaimes more killing then Ioues triple thunder, a 1000 deaths
     inhabit its point and edge wch all ways wait yʳ becke
     to offer bloudy sacrifises to yʳ furie.   [1015]
Pol: Very oportunely with this Ile make Lossarello meat for
     furies he shall know what it is to iniure kings.
ffar: 4 Receaue this purple mighty sir imbrodered ouer with
     ffairy diamonds, wch tho here in this low region they dis
     daine to shew ther lustre will when yᵒ once enter the con [1020]
     fines of yʳ fairy empire dart forth such a splendor that
     towring eagles will forget the sunne and come to trie
     ther young ones by their rayes.
ffar: 5 This sceptour great Politico giues yᵒ right to an em
     pyre whos limits the glorious eye of day that at one vew [1025]
     sees what this poore world can shew cold neuer yet
     discouer. ioyne Afric Asia Europ in one prouince
     and take in vast America to make vp its greatnes it
[Fol. 21] it will be no more compared with our vast empire then
     a nut shell with the world.   [1030]
ffar: 6 Now mighty prince we tender our allegiance to your
     greatnes and with bended knee desier to kisse the hand
     that sways the sceptor may command our liues and for
     tunes.

---

997 *his his*] read *his*
999 *rome*] a vertical stroke above the *r* appears to be the beginning of a capital *R*, abandoned in favor of the miniscule
1000 *thes*] *e* altered in the lt. br. ink from an *i*

[Fol. 20ᵛ]
1009 *prince*] *i* altered from some illegible letter, perhaps an *e*
1010 *wrought*] *o* altered from an *a*
1028-1029 *it it*] read *it*

THE FARY KNIGHT

    Scæna 6 enter [tow] 2 fairys singing   [1035]
    this song then 4 follows and begins
      A dance~

  1 Come ye faries come away
    Wait no more on Oberon
  2 ffor a glorious sunne doth sway   [1040]
    In your fary horison
  1 Let amorous Thetis now detaine
    Phœbus in her wauy bowers
  2 This radiant sunne which now doth raigne
    With purer light will [eer] ere be ours   [1045]
  1 Oberon hath left his throne [shining with]
    Shining with the richest gemms
  2 But it is no matter here is one
    Whos head was maid for diadems
  1 Se how the linked graces striue   [1050]
    In his face each to excel
  2 Whilst in the radiant orbs his eyes
    Do a 1000 Cupits dwell.

[Fol.21ᵛ] 1 The brightest safire is his skinne
    His nose is of the richest Ruby   [1055]
  2 Wher carbuncles may be sene
    Which speaks him plainely Bacchus to be.
  1 Vew vew how radiant emeralds shine
    One his head wch doth display,
  2 ffrõ fary diamons light diuine   [1060]
    And purer rays then doth the day.
  1 Come ye farys come away
    Salute yʳ king now newly crown'd
  2 Let this be a holly day [and with]
    And with sports and triumphs drown'd.   [1065]
  1 Come nimbly dance yʳ fary ring
    Tis ten to one but that it may be.
  2 A gratefull sight vnto your king
    To se how danceth euery fary.

1035 6] read 5   1046 [*shining with*]] erased

[Fol. 21]   [Fol. 21ᵛ]
 1040 *sunne*] *u* heavily written over what seems to   1058 *emeralds*] *l* heavily written over *ul*
  be an *o* and perhaps another illegible letter   1063 *newly*] *y* altered from dotted *i*
 1042 *1*] over *3*   1064 [*and with*]] erased
 1042 *amorous*] second *o* heavily written over an 1067 *be.*] read *be,*
  illegible letter

THE FARY KNIGHT

    The dance is then performed wch ended   [1070]
    They carry Polytico about the stage
    In triumph the rest singing
    As ffolloweth~

[Fol. 22]   *A Song*~

a ffar: Stand Phœbus stand in the enamld skey   [1075]
   And vew thes triumphs with thy glorious eye.
   Looke frõ the spangl'd valt and tel vs whether
   With triumphs great as thes was hurri'd thether.
   By his victorious eagles Ioue when in
   The Phlegon feilds the earth borne brood was sene [1080]
   fforc'd by his thunder in ther mother creepe
   Not daring once at heauen againe to peepe.
   Looke frõ thy goulden car and tel vs when
   With maiesty the king of Gods and men
   Æquall to this did in Olympus sway,   [1085]
   Or with more glory thou ere rulst the day.
Pol: Now now it is Ile make the Gods to know
   There rules a power as great as theirs below
   Plum'd victory shall to the enamel'd skey
   My chariots draw wher I with Ioue will trie,   [1090]
   Whos right it is to weare the stary crowne
   And tho' his surest lightning guard him downe
   This powerful arme shall throw the God and proue
   Me to the frighted world greater then Ioue.
            exeunt.   [1095]

[Fol.22ᵛ]   Enter Losserello in armer
      A drumb beaten before him
      His lance-prosade carring
       His sheald~

Los: Drumb againe none yet apeare for this contempt my [1100]
   sword shall cut more threads of liues then do the destinies. O

[Fol. 22]
 1075 *Phœbus*] an illegible letter has apparently been mended to form this digraph
 1076 *vew*] *v* written over an *lo* before the *e* was formed
 1080 *Phlegon*] *l* heavily mended, perhaps over an *e*
 1084 *Gods*] *G* altered from *g*
 1088 *theirs*] *i* undotted, but the reading is clear
 1089 *enamel'd*] *el* written over *le* and the apostrophe crowded in

[Fol. 22ᵛ]
 1092 *him*] read *him,*
 1098 *carring*] the letters have been considerably mended; apparently the original spelling was *carieng* and in the revision the first *r* was mended to delete the original *i*, the second *r* written over the original *e*, and the *i* written over the first minim of the original *n* which therefore remains imperfect

THE FARY KNIGHT

	I cold demolish whole mankind! a valior thus vnregua	
	rded. by my great hopes Ile open springs of bloud	
	shall drown'd the world in a crimson deluge. milia	
	ns of liues are to slight a sacrifise for my fury. here	[1105]
	after death shall forget to kil but by my sword wch	
	shall drinke more bloud of mortals then doth the ocean	
	riuers. Ile send at once so many soules to Stix shall	
	sinke ould Charons boat and make all after dispaire of	
	seing Elizium. dus yet none come. what lethergie	[1110]
	hath seased on mortals? or hath my looks wch beare	
	more terror then the Thracian Gods with a cold fea	
	re benumed all ther senses if it be so make the drumb	
	roar louder I will kil them with this feare.	
Lans:	Sir heare comes a champion	[1115]
Los:	O it semes they can be wak'd go both of you and somen	
	him to the fight tel him he shall haue the honour	
	to die by this heroicke hand~	

Enter Spendall~

Spen:	I am the valiants of all my company. they lie as	[1120]
[Fol. 23]	close yet as dormise. the loue of sacke hath ouercome	
	my feare and maid me hazard an eating by the giant to get	
	it. but who are thes? on my life the giants men Ile rune	
Drum:	Stay sir stay.	
Spen	O my vrgent occasions pray let me go my busines cals me.	[1125]
Lansp:	No busines can be of greater 'quens then that we come	
	about life and death lies on it.	
Spend:	O I am vndone!	
Drum	Not yet sir you may liue a quarter of an hower longer	
	Heare and tremble at what I haue to tel you. our great	
	master the mighty Losserello, whos very name strikes ter	[1130]
	ror in to mortals whos breathe is lightning and whos [w]	
	words are thunder daines to let you meet his puissent	
	arme in single cumbat. it will more enoble you to fall	
	by his hand then a 1000 pyramids of Corinthian brasse	[1135]
Spen:	Alas! sir it is amung my virtues not to be dangerously	

1104 *crimson*] the reading is uncertain; *o* was perhaps mended from an *e*
1108 *Stix*] *St* heavily written over two letters which are probably *le*
1113 *benumed*] *d* added in the dk. br. ink

[Fol. 23]
1121 *dormise*] the first minim of the *r* heavily mended over some illegible letter

1126 *No*] *N* altered from *n*
1127 *about*] read *about. Life*
1128 *vndone!*] exclamation mark altered from a colon
1129 *liue*] *u* over an illegible erasure
1130 *Heare*] *a* seems to be altered from an *e*
1132 *ror*] *o* altered from an *e*
1136 *be*] interlined above a caret in the lt. br. ink

THE FARY KNIGHT

              ambitious. wherefore beseech him to confer this [virtue] ho
              nour on an other both more desirous and worthy of it.
Drum: Come ther is no trifeling he is resolued you shall fight with
              him. Spen by this light I neuer dared yet to fight with any thing [1140]
              that had a tought in its head.
Lans: Harke he calls y° come away?
Spn   O I beseech you gentlemen plead for me
Drum Giue vs our fees then and we wil be your [layers] aduocats
              Iack scrach vp thy nymble perecranium his gould   [1145]
              must make vs eloquent
Spen: Here is for you and for you.
Lan: Is here all
[Fol.23ᵛ] Spen: No no ther is a reserue behind to put in your hand whi
              lst y° are pleading it wil make y° giue more emphice to   [1150]
              yʳ words.
Lans: Conten so we haue it.
Drum: Now kneele a suppliant whilst we start vp your
              nimbe-tung'd orators.
Lans: Most illustrious lend I beseech y° a fauorable eare to the   [1155]
              pittiful oration I am about to make (*aside*) (my hand
              is behind me why do y° not put? I shall not be able to
              to speake an other word else) this man whos vir
              tues accuses nature of cruelty for not furnishing him
              with more liues then one hauing bin so liberall as   [1160]
              to grant a lease of 9 to cats (*aside*) (hist my hand my
              hand why do not y°! that wch I am about to say will be
              worth it and it will not out else) is an humble peti
              tioner to y° for this one.
Los: Rech me my sheild Ile sacrifice him on that alter   [1165]
              of fortitude to the powerful god of war.
Spen: Oh ho! speake for me.
Lans Nay it is your on falt y° are so slow. how do y° thi | *he puts*
              nke I shold vnlesse you? what 2? this makes amens | *2 peeces*
              Stay mighty sir your puissant arme and take | *in his hand* [1170]
              not away that life wch saued will bring so large

1140 *Spen*] interlined above a caret
1141 *tought*] g and perhaps the second minim of the *u* heavily mended over an illegible letter
1143 *O*] altered from *I*
1143 *beseech*] h very closely resembles a k
1144 *fees*] s over an illegible letter
1144 *aduocats*] the deletion is made and *aduocats* added in the margin in the lt. br. ink
1145 *his*] h mended to delete the *t* of the original word *this*

1147 *Spen:*] over a four-letter word beginning with L and ending with d, probably *Land*
1148 *Lan:*] over a three-letter word beginning *Sp*, possibly *Spe* or *Spn*

[Fol. 23ᵛ]
1168 *slow*] sl over two illegible letters, perhaps *la*.
1168-1170 stage-direction added in the dk. br. ink
1169 *you*] the question mark follows *vnlesse*; *you* is interlined between above a caret

THE FARY KNIGHT

[Fol. 24]   a portion of glory to y°. for thinke I pray how
glorious it will be to se the grene oliue of clemency flo
rish amoung your victorious laurels. (*aside*) agai
ne againe I shall be out of breath elce.   [1175]

Drũ: I must begin sone or this rogue will get all. most re
nowned most refulgent most illustrious I se your
eyes and eares conuerted vpon me your poore oretor.
(hist. this way) whom not my merits but the iustnes
of the cause I am to plead cals to this honerable bar.   [1180]

Lanc   Sirrah peace and let y^r betters be heard before you

Drũ: (Hinder me not verlet) for vew this man vew him
I say frõ the top to the botome and y° shall find in him no
thing but worthy loue but worthy pity. his face wher
nature hath treasured vp all her riches will crey out of   [1185]
you if y° put him to death.

Spen: I by this light will it.

Drũ: Se his lookes se his nose so richly embelished with glow
ing rubies behould his cheaks hanging downe like bags
of nectare marke al the other parts of his body and   [1190]
heare them with a 1000 tungs telling y° if y° kill him y° dis
troy the most acomplished worke of nature and do a
deade will blast all your glory and pul æternall im
famy on your head.

Lanc: Peace thou impertinent thou obstreperous raskal   [1195]
I will only speake and only beheard in this place.

[Fol.24^v] Drũ   Renowned sir I hope y° will not permit such insolences
in the court at the barre in y^r heighnes presence. curb
I beseech y° his malepart tung.

Los: I charge y° silence.   [1200]

Lanc: Pox of his Rhetoricke he will get all.

Drũ: This trembling suppliant mighty sir as y° may well p
ceue is not descended of Cacus his race or the giant
brood against whom only y^r steele is [only] pointed and y^r swo
rd hath an edge. but one of human birth whos death   [1205[
if the thirst of bloud moue y° to. his good education can
bring y° to a place wher y° may extinguish it with
the richest wine Cicile can afford.

Spen: I by this light can I am acquainted with all the tau

[Fol. 24]
1181 *heard*] *e* altered from *a*
1183 *in*] interlined
1185 *of*] *o* closely resembles an *a*
1188 *lookes*] *s* added in the lt. br. ink
1188 *nose*] *se* crowded in in the lt. br. ink

[Fol. 24^v]
1197 *permit*] *e* heavily mended
1204 [*only*]] interlined above a caret in the ink
    of the text and deleted in the dk. br. ink
1206 *to.*] read *to,*
1209 *can*] read *can.*

THE FARY KNIGHT

ernes in the towne and know where the best Canary [1210]
is to be bought for mony.

Los: ffor this we grant the thy life and make the our
honourable prisoner. thy ransome shall be pay in
wine. sarrah bind you his hands, and do you beat
a dreadfull march before vs to giue the world notice [1215]
of our victory whilst I walke in triumph through
the streats.   exeunt.

        Scæna 7ᵃ enter Craft.
        And shift~

Craf: Thes picklocks will let yᵒ in to the closset do not faile [1220]
[Fol. 25] at the time appointed to haue al things in readines
I will be at the window with Snap to receaue them.
Shif: You know I am neuer negligent in thes affaires giue
but a whistle and I am for yᵒ.
Craf: Slid here comes Politico I will present you immediatly. [1225]

        Scæna 9 enter Politico.~

Pol: Dus not the earth bend vnder me? is it able to sustaine
such maiesty? O its proud to beare so great a monarke
se se it sends forth roses and violets to do me homage
and intice my stay. wher ere I go my presence makes a [1230]
spring. harke doth not each flower pclame me more
necesery then the sunne since at my absence with out
a killing frost they will hang downe ther silken heads
and dey tho sols most chering rayes shold force their
languishing spirit to inhabit their butiful body's. the [1235]
fragrant roses blush that ther sweets and beuty can
not retaine me, whilst lillies and violet grow pale
for greife that I will leaue them. but I must hast to
my blest kingdome wher the Gods themselues shall
enuey my happines and wish to change states with me. [1240]

1213 *pay*] read *payd*
1214 *bind*] *b* over an illegible letter, probably a *p*
1218 *7ᵃ*] read *8ᵃ*
1218 *Craft*] *C* altered from *c*
1220 *closset*] *l* heavily mended, probably over an illegible letter

[Fol. 25]

1227 *bend*] *b* perhaps altered from a letter which may have been *p*

1227 *me?*] question mark added in the dk. br. ink
1228 *maiesty?*] question mark altered in the dk. br. ink from a period
1234 *sols*] final *s* added in the lt. br. ink
1234 *rayes*] *r* heavily mended from an illegible letter
1236 *that*] *t* over an illegible letter, perhaps a *p*
1237 *violet*] read *violets*
1239 *shall*] probably by a slip of the pen the final *l* closely resembles an *h*

THE FARY KNIGHT

Craf: Stay mighty Oberon let not the pleasure of a kingdome
make y° forget Iustice wch the Gods do often leaue their
ambrosian faire to put in execution.   thinke it wil
[Fol.25ᵛ]   not be here after capital to wrong princes if Losse
rello goes vnpunished. [1245]

Pol: Losserelo!   this name hath rays'd an anger in me able
to distroy whole nature and fright the world to Chaos.
Losserello!   I wold forgo my right to fary land rather
then misse my reuenge.   O that he had as many liues as
heiers that my great anger might be satiated in killing [1250]
him.   I'le to him instantly tyme runnes on leaden whe
les til my reuenge be perfet.

Craf: Sir this fary shall conduct y° to the vserers house wher
Losserello will be with in this hower.

Pol: Tis to long to delay my fury but since it must be so I will [1255]
deuise the while to be an age in killing him lead the
way.

Craf You'l remember the time?

Shif: ffaile not y° and all is well.

Craf: Sir Ile go and make things ready for yʳ iurny to [1260]
ffaryland against your returne.

Pol: I prethe do.   Exeunt.

Scæna 10   enter Spendall and Losserello

Los: Three thousan art thou sure?

Spen: I three thousan I spoake with one that counted them. [1265]
[Fol. 26]   his iron club neer fell to the ground but hundereds
lay sprayling vnder it like mice.   some with out ar
mes or legs others with out heads.

Loss: If my spel make me [inuincible] victorious Ather
of Briton will be for got an Gey of Worwicke es [1270]
tem'd a cowerd to me, euery wher ther will be ballats
of my braue aduentures.   dust thinke he is there
yet?

Spen: To sure.

1241 *a*] interlined
1242 *Iustice*] *I* altered from *i*

[Fol. 25ᵛ]
1244 *here*] the first minim of the *r* deletes a letter, probably an *a*
1248 *rather*] initial *r* over another letter, perhaps a *t*
1249 *had*] *d* altered from *t*
1250 *my*] *y* altered from dotted *i*

1252 *wheles*] *w* possibly added later
1263 *Scæna*] *æ* altered from *e*

[Fol. 26]
1266 *fell*] *e* over *a*
1271 *to*] *t* heavily mended over an illegible letter, possibly an *f*
1272 *there*] the first minim of the *r* deletes an illegible letter, probably an *a*

THE FARY KNIGHT

Los: I feare the noyse of my warllicke drums hath [1275]
   made him retire.
Spen: O no cold that haue done it. we had triumph'd ere
   this and publicke thanks had bin pay'd vs by the citi
   zons for ther deleuery.
Loss: Wher lies he? [1280]
Spen: At Couets a vserers 2 streats of.
Los Lead the way to him he shall not out liue a [minite]
   minute.
Spen: Pardon vs mighty sir we are not weary of the
   liues y^o gaue vs. [1285]
Los: You raskal will you not? refuse and thou visits
   Pluto.
Spen: Oh sir!
      Scæna 11 enter Craft.

Craft: Health to the renowned Lossarello. [1290]
[Fol.26^v]Los: Art there Craft? I haue thought minuts years til I
   saw thee. by this light I haue [fout] fought with neuer a Giant
   since thou lefts me but this and my very looke ouer
   came him.
Spen: In dead it did it was so like a vizard it scar'd me. [1295]
Craf: Mighty sir the publicke safety implores y^r puissant
   arme to the conquest of a Giant whõ if your valior
   doth not defeite, with in this 2 houres will distroy
   the whole towne.
Los: Craft here is my hand Ile do it. I prethee bring me [1300]
   thether presently I shall grow rusty else for want of vse I
   haue bin like to mutany to or 3 times with in this quarter
   of an hower because I had none to fight with all. Craf: sir you
   must to my grannã first.
Loss: What to do? [1305]
Craf: To fecth a maieck sworde the diuil hath bin making for
   you this 3 days
Los: Tut I need none this and my spel is able to distroy an army
   of Giants al as great as Colburne.

1277 *it.*] read *it,*
1286 *raskal*] *k* written over *ca* and then *al* added
1289 *Scæna 11*] *æ* altered from *e*; second *1* over an illegible letter or figure which is perhaps *a*
1290 *Lossarello*] first *o* perhaps altered from an *a*

[Fol. 26^v]
1292 *fought*] interlined above a caret and the deletion; the stroke of deletion, the caret, and the correction made in the dk. br. ink
1293 *looke*] *e* in the dk. br. ink over an *s*
1294 *came*] *a* altered from *o*
1295 *did*] final *d* in the dk. br. ink over a *t*
1298 *2*] a heavy blot, probably accidental, follows this number
1302 *3*] over a straight stroke, perhaps the beginning of a *t*
1303 *Craf:*] interlined above a caret

THE FARY KNIGHT

Craf: Your spell wil do much that will keep y͡o frõ being hurt. [1310]
Los: And I care for no more.
Craf: But arm'd sir with this inchanted steele you [might] may me
 ete Mars in the feeld and make him crey quarter.
Los: Well Ile go fech it? wilt thou go with me?
Craf: No I can not my grannam hath sent me of an errant [1315]
 for the diuil Ile meet you at y͡r returne fare well.   exit Loss:
Craf: Snap art [thou] wher art thou?
Snap: Here here stand close I discouer light.

[Fol. 27]   Scæna 12 enter Shift with a
                Trunke vnder his arme and a   [1320]
                Light in his hand.

Shif: The siluer moone is downe, and night as not willing to be con
 scious to my theft hath sh[*]ut vp all her sterry eyes and clo
 sely bound them in with pichey clowds whilst frendly Mor
 pheus as if he were to sheare in the booty hath liberally   [1325]
 dispenc'd his soporeferus wan and sprinkl'd leathes iuce
 ouer the sleepeing eye brows of all the family. now
 were my ioys ꝑpleat if Craf and Snap were at hand. I'le
 whistle.
Snap: Tis shift. I heare his whistle. let vs to him.   [1330]
Craf: Content.
Shif: Come lads heare is an ample crop of goulden corne.
 Take this and this, here is all for wch the vserer hath
 damn'd himselfe a 1000 times.
Snap: ffor this I cold adore thee.   [1335]
Craf: We'l[e] haue thy stateu made in gould and tel the world
 it is Marcury.
Snap: This shall make vs se goulden days.
Craf: We'l dance til we turne aere.
Shif: Hast home with it and send Losserello presently to his [1340]
 Giant or I shall dance wher I am loath in a rope at
 the Gallace. — Snap: he shall be with thee instantly.   exeunt

---

1312 *may*] *might* deleted and *may* interlined above in the lt. br. ink
1314 *Los: Well Ile go fech it*] apparently first omitted and then crowded in in a smaller hand but with a pen as fine pointed as the text at this place; the question mark and the rest of the line were added with a much heavier quill
1315 *not*] *t* altered from another letter, perhaps an *r*

[Fol. 27]
1326 *wan*] read *wand*
1328 *Snap*] over *Shifte*
1330 *heare*] *are* heavily written over some illegible letters, the first minim of the *r* being formed over an original *e*
1336 *We'l[e]*] final *e* erased and the *l* mended
1336 *stateu*] *eu* over a partially erased letter which may be a *y*

THE FARY KNIGHT
Actus Quintus

[Fol.27ᵛ]   Scæna prima~

       Enter Losserello with his Lance-prosade   [1345]
       And drummer~

Los: So with this I do defie the whole world. mortals shall
feare no longer Ioues idle thunder but my frowne, when
I but stamp fright'd nature shall hide her selfe and the Gods
frõ ther starry mansion lookeing downe at the vniuer   [1350]
sal disorder of things shall behould one that dare oppose
ther Ioue tho arm'd with his best lightning. what is not
Craft here yet? how dares he thus forfit his life by ma
keing me expect?

Lanspro: He is arriu'd.   [1355]

Craf: Illustrious sir writ your selfe in crimson charecters of bloud
with that yʳ all confunding steele in the booke of fame
it will be glorious to haue yʳ name blowne by her trum
pet to the fary region before you.

Los: As thou tenderst mankind lead me to the Giant for   [1360]
a minuts delay will make me turne all to nothing
I shall demolish men wemen and children if I
fight not instantly.

[Fol.28] Craft: Sir here is the house giue vs leaue to be gon we
dare not vew the combat.   exunt.   [1365]

Drum: Pray sir let me go to the Giant will scare me out of my lit
tle wits.

Loss: Leaue the drum and be gon you cowerd you are not
fit company for my valiant selfe. what are they all
gon. by this life I cold fiend in my hart to be gon to I am   [1370]
horriblely afraid flesh will be flesh I can not chose but tremble tho' I
be hang'd when I go to fight. for who knows but this giant   [shold
may be enchanted to and then we may fight our harts out
and not hurt on an other. besids he may take me pri
soner and hang me. what a blockehead was I not to   [1375]
excepet the gallace. I thinke it is safest when all is
done to runne away, but so I shall vtterly loose my
hopes in fary land king Oberon will neuer looke at
me whell when the worst comes to the worst he can

[Fol. 27ᵛ]
  1348 *idle*] *i* over the downstroke for a *t*

[Fol. 28]
  1366 *to*] read *too,*

1371 *flesh will be flesh*] interlined above a caret in the lt. br. ink
1376 *excepet*] *et* over a *t* probably before the next word was written

THE FARY KNIGHT

	not hurt me. Ile venter to giue an allarum.	[1380]
	he beats the drume	
Poll:	ffary looke out. what is the matter.	
Loss:	Descend thou giant thou broud of Cacus and enter com bat with renouned Losserello this martial hand shall proue the a villan.	[1385]
Shif:	O it is my master y° call vpon he shall be with y° imme diatly. sir here is Losserello come to fight with you.	
Pol:	Looke out againe and se whether thou dust not discouer armed men with him.	

[Fol.28ᵛ] Los: Thou terræ filius wilt thou not obay my summons ether [1390]
hide thy selfe in thy mother earth from my fury or this this
powerful arme of mine shall cut the in to attomes and strow
her with them that she may fertiliz'd with thy viper bloud
shout vp a crop of giants wch my sworde in like ma
ner shall mow downe.   O my fury how it bowiles I'le [1395]
breake this Poliphemian den and in and kil the fea
reful monster.

Shif: Your grace heares what he sayes.   he will breake in
vpon vs.

Pol: Giue me my sworde I come I come to send him to the [1400]
Stygian lacke ther to be meat for furies.

Loss: He is comeing.   what a rogue was I to prouoke him
thus?   I cold fiend in my hart to runne away now.

Scæna 2°   enter Pollitico.

Pol: Thou hads better haue bestrid a billow when the angre north [1405]
plows vp the sea or made Ioues fire thy foode then thus
haue cald an angre great as mine to thy distruction.
my eyes dart lightning and my ful swollen rage like the
heigh wrote sea is ready to ouer whelme the with a
deluge of deaths. [1410]

Los: By this light what will become of me.   if I were not
inchanted what a pickle shold I be in now?   wel I per
[Fol. 29] ceue thou art valiant I will not cut of so much che
uelry at a blow thou shall liue and only be my prisoner
thou shalt efaith come I will vse the honorablely. [*]~ [1415]

Pol: Villan. I will hew the in to as many parts as I haue tow
nes in faryland wch I will cause to be hung vp in them
an æternal monument of my iustice on traytors.

[Fol. 28ᵛ]
1405 *north*] added in the margin

[Fol. 29]
1415 the decoration deletes a letter, probably the start of another word

THE FARY KNIGHT

Los: Nay then I must fight tho it be but for my hanches Poli
pheme heare and tremble. with this dreadful steele [1420]
I will cut thee in to collops and send them to the furies
for a breake fast.

Pol: This this shall poast thy blacke soule ther to be whipp'd [by]
with vipers by Tisiphone.
        they fight Pollitico fals. [1425]
Oh I fall I fall. braue Losserello take my sword and
and let it be thy glory to haue ouercome in fight mig
hty Pollito Ile pay my ransome a princes ransome
a 1000 bushels of diamons and pearele beside 1000000
acres in faryland. Ile giue the a prouince to rule [1430]
in of such extent that Phæbus mounted in his flameing
chariot cold neer oer looke it and yet retaine a king
dome for my selfe.

Los: I haue a monstrous mind to kill him I neer kild any
body in my life the boyes will not thinke me valiant [1435]
elce. sirrah let me tie thy hands behind thee.

Pol: I beseech y^o vse me more noblely I am a royall pri
[Fol.29^v] soner I am a king.

Los: Thou art a giant.

Pol: No I protest sir not I. [1440]

Los: What deerst thou lie in my presence? giue me your
hands preasently Or.

Pol: O for euer Phæbus dwel in Thetis bosome. let æternal
night inhabit here to couer my disgrace.

Los: Come put thy head in. [1445]

Pol: I beseech you sir.

Los: Dare you rebel?

Pol: Oh no.

Los: Ile hang thee vp immediatly.

Pol: Let me die a more noble death. [1450]

Los: No it is more for my honour to hang thee.

Pol: And must I then be hang'd O cursed faite!

Los: Because thou art no giant I'le make thee streach til
thou art one.

Pol: Alas what a proper man is cast away. [1455]

1429 *1000000*] last two cyphers added in the dk. br. ink

[Fol. 29^v]

1442 *preasently*] a stroke which may be the beginning of a question mark follows this word

1443 *Thetis*] *T* altered from *t*

1449 *imediatly*] initial *i* written heavily over an illegible letter

1453 *giant*] *n* written over an original *t*, and then a new *t* added before the next word was written

[45]

THE FARY KNIGHT

Los: Leaue prating sirrah and bid adew to the world for now
I hoist thee vp.

Pol: Oh hold let me haue the right of the gallas and sing a
psalme before I die.

Los: Thou shut, thou shut. Ile put thee to death legaly. [1460]

   Pol: Draw neare good people all I say
       And lissen to my woe

[Fol. 30]
   That you may not become a pray
       As I am to my foe.
   I that of late. was crowned king [1465]
       And caried in great state
   Must in a hempten halter swinge
       Repentance comes to late.
   ffare well my crowne and sceptor eke
       ffare well my Royall throne [1470]
   ffor if Politico you seake
       Woe is me he can not come.
   A hempten halter holds him in
       Lossarello hath decreed,
   That he shall dancing in a string [1475]
       Be choaked with necke weade.
   Ye faries whersoer you be
       To se me post away
   ffor if you hast not this is he
       That straight your prince will slae. [1480]
   My louing Subiects euery one
       Take this my last commande

[Fol.30ᵛ]
   To se me vnder a marble stone
       Buried in fary land.
   To this I adde that when you come [1485]
       At mide night for your foode
   You pinch Losserello to the bone
       ffor sheding of my bloud.

Los: Thou Raskall. is it for this I haue let the liue thus long? thou
shalt not speake an other word. [1490]

enter Snape

Pol: Oh ho!

1458 *and*] *n* written over an original *s* and then
a *d* added before the next word was written
1459 *psalme*] *s* over an illegible letter
1461 *Draw*] *a* over *e*

[Fol. 30]
1474 *hath*] *t* over *o*

1481 *Subiects*] *S* altered from *s*

[Fol. 30ᵛ]
1489 *Raskall*] *s* over *sc*
1489 *long?*] question mark crowded in after the next word was written
1492 *Oh*] *O* altered from *I*

THE FARY KNIGHT

Snap: Stay the execution I command you in Oberons name
Pol: A repriue a repreuiue.
Los: Who art thou that dares hinder Iustice? [1495]
Snap: If yᵒ be the braue Losserello I summon yᵒ to the fary cort
    ther to be honoured by Oberon for the good seruice you
    haue done our state.~ ~ ~ ~ ~ ~ ~ ~ ~ ~ ~
    And this your prisoner whõ I cite to the barre to answer
    as a delinquent articles of hie treason we charge him [1500]
    with.
Los: May not I hang him first?
Snap No it is Oberons command he shold be brought aliue
Los: Let vs march forwerd then.
Pol: Alas what wil become of me? this is out of the frieing [1505]
    pan in to the fier.   Exeunt.

    Scæna 3ᵃ   enter Shift and Couet~

[Fol.31] Shif: Theues, theues, theues.
Couet: Ha! what is the matter?
Shif: O sir the saddest night that euer came. here hath bin Spend [1510]
    al, who hath brought a champion to incounter my master
    the fight was terrible and doutfull victory with snowy wings
    long houered ore the champians heads. at last blind ffortune
    gaue the palme to Losserello who hauing taken my master
    prisoner fell to pilleging. he broke open a closet going in to [1515]
    the paller.
Cou: My counting house   O I am vndone!
Shif: Whence he tooke a great bag with a trunke. they sem'd wai
    ty I beleue ther was some thing in them.
Cou: Some thing? all that I haue swet for this 30 yeare. O [1520]
    I am vndone.
Shift: Alas sir!
Cou: I can not outliue my greife.
Shif Tis well.   [he fiends a hal[te]
Cou: Haue they left me this? this then shall witnes I [ter.~   [1525]
    of the deare gold.   [die for loue

1495 *art*] originally *at*; the original *t* altered to *r* and a new *t* added before the next word was written
1497 *Oberon*] O mended from some illegible letter
1503 *Oberons*] O mended from some illegible letter
1504 *Let*] *t* altered from *d*
[Fol. 31]
1512 *doutfull*] originally *doufu*; *t* written over the original *f*, a new *f* formed over the first minim of the original final *u*, and finally a new second minim added to this *u* and *ll* added before the next word was written
1512 *with*] the first minim of the *w* apparently written over the start of another letter
1524-1525 stage-direction added in the lt. br. ink
1526 *gold*] *l* heavily mended, apparently to delete a preceding *u*

THE FARY KNIGHT

Shif: You'l not be iust and hang y^r selfe? will you?
Cou: Let me alone and se.
Shif: Sir y° shall command my helping hand to this good worke
     if y° please. [1530]
Cou: O it is the last office y° can do a distressed man.
Shif: Come sir Ile put the rope about your necke. I am content to
     [be your executioner] pleasure so much your naibors as to be y^r ex-
Coue: Thanks gentle shift. [cutioner.
[Fol.31^v]Shif: They will thanke me I am confident they loue y° so well. y° [1535]
     need not say y^r prayers it will be but time lost.
Coue: Right right hoist me vp when thou wilt.
Shif: Now then yet take this comfort before you die thos that rob'd
     y° are in [hol] hold and the monies safe in a iustices hand.
Cou: Ha! this is a repriue thes words make me liue againe, tho [1540]
     I had one foote in [the graue] heauen I shold step backe to se my belo
     ued gold. come shift to the iustices with me minuts are yea
     res till I recouer my losse.
Shif: What a rogue was I to let him loose. wel I haue a plot in
     my head to make him hang him selfe when he hath not me to [1545]
     help him. com sir.
Cou: I come I come the desier to se my gold wil make me out strip
     eagles in ther flight.

          Scæna 4^a *enter Craft like*
          The king of faries waited [1550]
          On by 4 Peares~

ffar 1 We are to sone, they are not yet arriu'd.
Craf: Tis no mater. we do not put on the habits of kings euery day
     We'le practise til they come to behaue our selues with more
     maiesty. each of y° I hope knows my titles: mighty Oberon [1555]
     king of ffaryes, lord of the Antipodes and great Eutopia
[Fol. 32] haue a care the profane name of Craft fall not frõ you.
     remember the congies and the distance ye must oberue with
     the other ceremonies I haue spent 4 howers sweat to make
     y^r plumbeus intelects capable of. [1560]
ffar 2 My stately king of pigmies we know all ad vnguem that is
     to a haire.
Craf: Bring the chaire of state and keepe the order I put you
     in when we practiz'd last.

[Fol. 31^v]
1539 [*hol*]] crossed out after an accidental blot over *ol*

1541 *heauen*] interlined in the lt. br. ink above the deletion made in the same ink
1547 *out*] *o* very heavily mended
1553 *kings*] *s* added in the dk. br. ink

THE FARY KNIGHT

        Scæna 5 enter 2 faries with Losserello   [1565]
        Polletico and Spendall~

Snap: The court is sat his maiesty is ther. dread leage y^r comma
nd is perform'd.
Craf: Are they arriu'd?
Snap: They are?   [1570]
Craf: Which is my friend Losserello?
Los: Here and it please y^r maiesty.
Craf: A man of a promising countinance and of a backe big enuf
to beare all the fary honers we can confer.
Snap: Knele downe and present y^r selfe his grace is almost in lo   [1575]
ue with you.
Los: Illustrious Oberon tho mortals dazel'd with the faire splendor
of my virtues stile me mighty stile me renoun'd Losserello
yet the highest honour my ambition soers to is to be counted
your vassel. this puissant arme wch with in this 3 howers hath   [1580]

[Fol.32^v] hath distray'd more giants and dragons then all the enchan
ted knights frõ king Athors time vpwards is only power
ful when it wealds a sword in y^r quarrel. at y^r command mighty
prince it deare grapple with Ioue tho Mars did help him.
this pigmy giant wch now you se [heare] here a trembling   [1585]
suppliant (knele sirrah) was once with in this halfe hower 3 as big as Col
burne. his head iustld the stars and threatned the Gods with
a new war. his eyes wer as big as busshils and he spit mo
re fire in a quarter of an hower then the burning drake
Sir Lacelot du laceke fought with did in a yeare. his iron club was
not to be borne with 5000 oxen. yet in lesse then an hou   [1591]
wers fight I made him stoope. beleue me sir at euery
blow I cut of more superfluus flesh then wold haue made a 1000
lusty beafe eators. at last with offen paring him I brought
him to this passe y^o se him in. tho before he was eleuen   [1595]
times higher then the element. sirrah is not not all
this trew? say no and Ile make thee no bigger then
a squerrel.
Pol: O I dare not I confesse he ouercame me.
Los: I and brauely to did I not?   [1600]
Craf: I can for bare no longer mighty Losserello receaue

[Fol. 32]
  1578 *Losserello*] second *l* over an *o*
  1579 *soers*] *e* altered from an illegible letter, perhaps an *a* or *u*

[Fol. 32^v]
  1582 *Athors*] *t* heavily mended and broadened at the base so as to delete what was apparently a preceding *r*
  1586 *(knele sirrah)*] interlined above a caret
  1588 *big*] *b* heavily written over an illegible letter
  1590 *fought with*] interlined above a caret
  1593 *made*] interlined above a caret in the lt. br. ink

THE FARY KNIGHT

        some part of the reward thy braue deads haue
        merited.
                Crafte draws his sworde

      Los: Oh I beseech your maiesty.   [1605]
[Fol.33] Craf: Come Losserello thou art modest. do not refuse.
      Los: O pardon me sir I haue not liu'd long enouffe the desti
            nes haue decreed more giants shall fall by my hand
            before I die.
      Craf: Die Losserello?   thou shalt liue and liue til thy heirrs   [1610]
            be siluer and grene againe with laurels. thy faire vir
            tues deserue it.
      Los: Put then vp y^r dreadfull steele it makes me tremble
            more then mine did giants.
      Craf: I must honoure the with it first.   {*he knights him*}   [1615]
      Los: Oh oh!
      Craf: Rise vp sir Losserello del fumo fary knight of the
            cornu copia bring out the habilliments of his ordor.
      Los: O was it to knight me I feard some thing else when
            I saw the sword. {*a fary brings in a pare of hornes*}   [1620]
      Craf: Before thes sacred antlers touch thy brow sweare to
            be faithfull.
      Los: I do mighty Oberon.
      Craf: And not to hold any thing terrene that may deroga
            te from the dignity we inuest thee with.   [1625]
      Los: No as I am a knight of the hornes will I not.
      ffar: Of the cornu copia say.
      Los: O must they be cal'd by that name. Ile remember it next
            time. I haue an it please your grace a little durty earth
[Fol.33^v]   wch in the lower region yealds me a 1000 pound a   [1630]
            yeare wch I am resolued to shake of with my morta
            lity and giue it to a fary wich for a fauor I receaued
            frõ her I beleue your grace is acquainted with the di
            uil pray giue him thes writings to carry to his dam
            the wich.   [1635]
      Craf: I will and now I creat thee earle of Eutopeia gene
            ral of all my sea forces at the antipodes giue me

---

1605 *beseech*] *s* heavily mended over an illegible letter

[Fol. 33]

1610 *heirrs*] second *r* written over what may be the start of an *s*

1611 *siluer*] *i* over an illegible letter which may be an *s*

1615 stage-direction and bracket added in the lt. br. ink

1617 *fumo*] *o* heavily mended, perhaps over an illegible letter

1620 brackets added in the lt. br. ink

1625 *the dignity*] *e* of *the* heavily mended to delete a following *s*; *d* of *dignity* may be written over some other letter, and *g* is altered from a *d*

1628 *cal'd*] *l* is blotted from *ll*

[50]

THE FARY KNIGHT

	the antlars to fix them to his brow.
Los:	O how my ioys do swel me. I shall burst.
Craf:	Bring a chare Losserello set downe and beare a part [1640]
	in condemning of a traitor thy mighty arme hath
	subdued. barrester lay out his accusation.
Bar:	Pollitico! hold vp thy hand at the bar, guilty or not
	guilty?
Pol:	Not guilty. [1645]
Bar:	Pollitico thou art a traitor a villan a rat of Nilus
	and thus I proue it.
Los:	I marry is he ticle him vp brauely and I wood thou wert
	hang'd if thou best not spiteful.
Bar:	Most illustrious and you reuerend iudges who has as ma [1650]
	ny eyes as siluer haers to discouer treason open them
	all I beseech you and vew the most execrable traitor
	the [world] sune eer saw. this this is he for whos treason one
	world is not sufficient [but] [for] for after he had [suffe] subuerted
	the states [by hi] of princes by his [wiles] plots and con [1655]

[Fol. 34] spirices in the lower region, dared (what dares
not traitors?) giant like streach out his hand against
the gods.

Los:	Nay Ile assure you he is a giant take him for what
	yᵒ will. [1660]
Bar:	Dared I say attempt the sacr'd person of our prince
	and with damnable treason vnderminding our state ende
	uor the blowing vs vp with our wiues and children
	in to the moone that he with his vipor brood might
	come and inhabit our blessed region. [1665]
Pol:	Mighty prince and you my lords.
Bar:	Peace traitor your lordships will fiend him very im
	pudent. but seing this serpentine treason chrush'd in
	the shel, pricke vp yʳ eares I beseech you fauorable
	iudges and lissen to his second attempt far more enormi [1670]
	ous then the former. for in this he plainely shewed him
	selfe a wich a nicromanser a diuil taking by art ma

[Fol. 33ᵛ]
  1640 *Craf:*] *r* over what may be an *h*
  1646 *Pollitico*] *c* over a *t*
  1653 *sune*] interlined above the deletion
  1654 [*for*]] interlined above deleted *but* and then deleted in turn
  1654 *for*] interlined above *after*

[Fol. 34]
  1657 *like*] *i* over erased *y*

  1662 *vnderminding*] *ing* interlined above a caret
  1663 *uor*] *r* over an erased letter, perhaps *g* or *y*
  1666 *my*] *y* altered from dotted *i*
  1667 *lordships*] originally begun *lorsh*; then a *d* was written over original *s*, an *s* over original *h*, and *hips* added before the next word was written
  1672 *taking*] *i* apparently written over an *e*

THE FARY KNIGHT

        ieck the sacred pson of mighty Oberon deluding ma
        ny of his honest subiecks by this imposture O crime not
        to be expiated by torments!   [1675]
Pol: Sirs I beseech you let me speake for my selfe.
Bar: This this my lords condemnes him he wold speake for
        him selfe. this alone makes him guilty of treason. for [he]
        who knows not but he who wold defend a traitor is guilty
        of treason. but thou Pollitico desiring to speake for   [1680]
        thy selfe being a traitor wolds defend a traitor. therfore

[Fol.34^v]   thou art guilty of treason and deserues (as your gra
        uities reuerend iudges know) to die by all the racks wheles
        brasen buls can be inuented or found out. vew him now
        conscripted fathers and tel me whether he looks not li   [1685]
        ke a traitor.
Los: I by this light doth he [like a man]
Bar: Like a man made vp of bloud of murther of rapine
        se se inraged fury sits in his forehead and marks
        vs out for slaughter. his eyes too fire brands already   [1690]
        menace distruction to this stately place behold they
        begin to spread abroad ther flames his nose is afire
        vew how it glowes. we shall be all burnt if present
        execution dispach not the traitor.
Los: Slid call for some water fling it vpon him presently   [1695]
        to preuent the danger.

                Scæna Sexta

             Enter Couet and Shift.

Shif: That is he wch sits by the iustice with the rams hor
        nes.   [1700]
Cou: I'le atteach him presently least he escape. gentle men
        rome for a plaintife.
Craf: What is the matter?
Cou: I charge this man of fellony, lay hold of him I com
        mand you in the kings name.   [1705]
Craf: What bold mortal is this that dares?
[Fol.35] Cou: Iustice you are here to se the laws executed let this man

---

1673 *ieck*] the *e* apparently written over a *t*
1679 *who*] interlined above a caret in the lt. br. ink
1680 *Pollitico*] P altered from *p*

[Fol. 34^v]
1690 *too*] final *o* crowded in in the dk. br. ink

1695 *Slid*] *i* may have been crowded in later
1702 *rome*] *r* over an erasure, perhaps of *R*
1703 *What*] W over O

[Fol. 35]
1707 *the*] interlined in the dk. br. ink

THE FARY KNIGHT

	go at your peril.	
Los:	Dus he accuse me of fellony? giue me rome stand frõ betwene vs. I'le tosse him.	[1710]
Craf:	Hold mighty Losserello sombody lay hold of the madman	
Cou:	You'l make me mad if you vse me thus, my house broake open and the malefactor —	
ffa:	Sir wher are you?	
Cou:	Wher the laws shold be put in execution against the ues. but it semes Mr Iustice is a shearer in the booty. well Ile go to heigher powers Ile make him answer it at the sessions.	[1715]
ffa:	This fellow talks streangly. do you know wher you are?	[1720]
Cou:	No wher am I?	
ffa:	In the fary court in the presence of Oberon whõ you vse thus contemptable.	
Cou:	O my stars! what diuil hath brought me hether? let me go home and die in peace.	[1725]
ffa:	No sir y° must be pinch'd to death by fary elues for y^r rudenes showen in court.	
Cou:	O cursed shift wher hast thou brought me!	
Craf:	Pul out his tung. is he not yet silent?	
ffa:	Not a silable or —	[1730]
Craf:	My lords your wisdomes are by this suffiently infor m'd of the enormity of this malefactors crime. pro cede to sentence let euery one deliuer a part that we may fiend out some exquisit torment to kill him by.	

[Fol.35ᵛ]

1	Hang him.	[1735]
2	Its to slight a torment.	
3	Burne him.	
4	It will dispach him to sone we must be an age in killing him.	
5	fflea him	[1740]
1	That is to common a death.	
2	What thinke y° of cutting of his legs and making him ride the brasen bull?	
3	Its not in fasshon.	

1709 *fellony?*] question mark apparently crowded in later
1712 *You'l*] u over a partially erased l
1719 *do*] d over some letter, perhaps an i
1721 *am*] a over an erased I
1721 *I?*] question mark added in the dk. br. ink, perhaps over an erased question mark which had been too far below the line for clarity

1724 *stars!*] exclamation mark added in the dk. br. ink
1730 *silable*] second l very heavily blotted, perhaps over some other letter
1732 *enormity*] e altered from i

[Fol. 35ᵛ]
1735 *Hang*] H altered from h

THE FARY KNIGHT

Los: Cut a hole in one leg and put the other through it [1745]
and make him dance Caranto through faryland.
4 That is most dreadful.
Los: If it [**] be not to great a punishment let me be his executio
ner Ile tos him to death one my brow antlars.
Craf: Pollitico thou deseruest greater torments then are yet na [1750]
med. but Ile be marciful thou shalt bey thy life for a
some of ready mony.
Pol: Illustrious Oberon my whole estate wer it as great
as yours [it] wold be to little to redeme me frõ the tor
ments they haue named. [1755]
Craf: Ile be content with a 1000 or so pay'd ready downe
Pol: Your maiesty shall haue 5 it was the whole summe
I receau'd for my land I lately sold.
3. What made yͦ sel your land senior?
4. O sir he intended to giue a [recreation] treat to the fary elues [1760]
at his entrance to Oberons throne.
[Fol.36] Pol: Do not ripe vp old wounds I intended to do some thing.
Craf: Pollitico send for the monies presently this fary knows
your house he shall fecth it. giue him your kees with
a derection wher to fiend it. [1765]
Pol: In a closet going out of the hall yͦ shall fiend alittle tru
ncke, the heauines will tel yͦ it is frought with gold.
Spen: Illustrious Oberon before this honorable assembly rise. I
beg [you] iustice against this vserer who hath not only af
fronted yor noble friend Losserello accusing him of fello [1770]
ny but also doth most iniuriously detaine monies dew
to me for land he bought.
Craf: Officers procede to iustice. Couet hold vp thy hand at
the barre
Shif: Sir he begs the marcy of the court. that he may haue [1775]
leaue to go home and hang [my] him selfe.
Cra: He shall after we haue done with him.
Bar: Answer. guilty or not guilty?
Cou: Not guilty.
Cra: Call in the elues (*enter elues*) pinch him til he confes. [1780]
Elu: Ti ti ta ti
Cou: Oh ho guilty guilty.
Cra: Wher are the writings?

1748 [**]] the letters now illegibly deleted in the
    dk. br. ink were interlined
1748 *not*] interlined in the dk. br. ink
1756 *ready*] *y* over *ie*

1760 *treat*] interlined in the lt. br. ink above the
    deletion made in the dk. br. ink
[Fol. 36]
1776 *him*] interlined above the deletion

THE FARY KNIGHT

Cou:	I know not. Craf will he not confes? pinch him againe	
Elues	Ti ti ta ti ti	[1785]
Cou:	In my bosome, in my bosome.	
Cra:	Pul then out.	
[Fol.36ᵛ] Cou:	I shall pul out my hart then they are fastn'd to it.	
Cra:	Its no matter. out with them (*Couet puls them out*) Spendall take the writings. recorder fine him 6000 pounds for the insolences he hath shwen in court.	[1790]
Cou:	Ile die first.	
Cra:	Pinch him to death elues.	
Elu:	Ta ti ti Ta ti ti (*they pinch him.*)	
Cou:	Oh ho I will I wil.	[1795]
Cra:	Bring pen and inke imediatly that he may put his hand and seale to thes writings that shall oblige him to the payment of the monies. recorder se it done. crier in the meane while proclame our ordinance for the purchasing of lands.	[1800]
Cry:	O yes! O yes! O yes! any man or woman that weary of mortality wold transplant them selues in to great Oberons kingdome let them forthwith apeare and for 100 pounds pay'd downe they shall haue a 1000 pounds a yeare entailed vpon them and ther heiers for euer in fary land.	[1805]
Cra:	What none apeare?	
Shif:	Yes yʳ maiesty hath a chapman Spendall will pur chase.	
Craf:	Hast thou a mind to leaue this foggy climat and inhabit the fortunat ilands wher planty hath layed vp all her store wch to this lower world she hands out in in parcels. speake.	[1810]
[Fol.37] Spen:	And it please your grace ther is but one difficulty holds me backe.	[1815]
Craf:	What is that?	
Spen:	Is ther the life of man ther? is ther sacke? if this be wanting tho al things elce conspire to make the place happie it will afford me but a wreched banishment.	

1784 *Craf*] interlined above a caret in the dk. br. ink
1785 *ti*] final *ti* heavily written over two illegible letters
1786 *in my*] *y* written over a dotted *i*
1787 *then*] read *them*
[Fol. 36ᵛ]
1794 *they*] *y* added in the lt. br. ink

1796 *inke*] *k* over *c*
1805 *heiers*] the reading uncertain; it appears that the second *e* was written over an original *r*, the following *r* over an original *s*, and a new final *s* added
1808 *chapman*] *p* heavily mended, perhaps to delete a preceding letter

THE FARY KNIGHT

Cra: The richest wines of Grece are water compared with the [1820]
 diuine liquor this place affords. it is the vineyard of the
 gods each tree is frought with nector wch Ganemede doth
 gather in ful bowles for Ioues one drinking. ther is not
 a spring but powers forth wine pore mortals here wold gi
 ue ther liues to tast. [1825]

Spen: Mighty Oberon not stored with monies take thes writings
 in this lower region they are worth [th**] thousans containing
 the right to a Lordship as great and rich as any is in Cicily.

Craf: Content we take them. secretary giue him a bil to receaue
 10000 pounds a yeare in fary land. [1830]

ffa 2 Sir the fary hath brought the truncke with Politico's gold.

Cra: Treasurer let it be your charge to se it safe. are the vse
 rers writings made and sign'd?

ffa 4. They are with much ado he swounded twice whilst he writ
 his name and seal'd them. [1835]

Craf: Alas! Ile comfort him againe presently. my lords it be
 comes my greatnes to be magnificent. wherfore least
 thes mortals shold repine at ther transitory losses. first
 on Couet I confer 100000 pounds a yeare with the title
 of Lord [Ch****] cheife iustice of fary-land. [1840]

[Fol.37ᵛ] Cou: [A] 100000 pound a yeare thes words wold fech me out of
 my graue if I were buried. I fiend ther force all ready.
 ther very sound hath inspir'd a sprightly vigor through
 my whole body. I feele youthfull bloud dancing a sprightly
 measure through my weathered vaines, wch [g] age and [1845]
 labor had dried vp. I am young againe. O great Obe
 ron what thanks are dew? am I the first that shall
 writ noble of my famely? shall the Autum of my age
 proue a florishing spring of glory to my race? O I am ra
 uished out of my selfe! [1850]

Cra: Couet lord cheife iustice of fary land take yʳ place in
 court.

Los: Not before me you Iew! vnlesse yᵒ will tast my fatal steel.

Cou: Keepe the peace and offer not violence to a man of honer
 his maiesties priuy counseler, least the cold hand of iusti [1855]
 ce seize vpon you.

Los: Stand not before me then.

[Fol. 37]
 1839 *100000*] final *o* crowded in, perhaps as a later addition

[Fol. 37ᵛ]
 1843 *inspir'd*] *d* over an illegible letter

1844 *whole*] first minim of the *w* written over an upright stroke, perhaps the start of a *b*

1849 *florishing*] first minim of the *r* was written to delete a *u*

THE FARY KNIGHT

Cra: You Spendall for your loue to sacke we creat you lord
of all our Canary Ilands take your place in court now
my lords I hope ther is not a mortal present but   [1860]
hath pertaken of my bounty.

Pol: Except Politico whos pardon will make him for
euer proclame your clemency.

Craf: And thou Politico shall not complaine of my liberality

[Fol. 38] I'le satisfie the height of thy desier and what treason   [1865]
cold not bring thee to my bounty shall confer vpon thee.
    Come set thee then vpon my throne
    I do inuest thee Oberone.
    On thy head I put my crowne,
    On thy backe my purple gowne,   [1870]
    Whilst my selfe I do become
    Honest Craft not Oberone. ha ha ha!

Pol: Ha!

Spen: Thus cosn'd?

Cou: Do I dreame?   [1875]

Los: All my honours drap of on a suddaine?

Cra: Nay wounder not fary Lords. you see Oberon that was. y^o se
Oberon that is. go ye with him to y^r hopes in faryland. Ile be con
tent to make my fortunes here, wch will be compleat if
Sirs your smile and pardon for this long trial of y^r pa   [1880]
tience approue the getting.   *Exit Craf cũ socijs*

Cou: O let me die in this goulden dreame!

Pol: Am I thus guld cheatd both of my mony's and honours?
Ile mount a turne-vp cart and preach til the end of the
world.   [1885]

Los: O this Cursed Craft! I begin to doubt my enchantment.
come follow I'le lead you to your reuenge

Spen: Come away.

[Fol.38^v] Pol: Couet is in a swond.

Spen: Wake him   [1890]

Cou: No let me die that my ghost may hant him euerlastingly.

Spen: Come get vp let vs purshew reueng whilst anger swels our vaines.

Cou: I come I come this word reueng hath made me strong as
Hercules. O reueng!
    Exeunt omnes.   [1895]

1862 *Politico*] *co* very heavily blotted
1862 *him*] *h* over an *f*
[Fol. 38]
1872 *ha ha ha!*] added in the lt. br. ink

1878 *with him*] interlined above a caret in the dk. br. ink
1881 *approue*] second *p* over an *r*

THE FARY KNIGHT

Epeloge~

Let Poits, sir, to Apollo's wreth aspire
And be acounted of the muses quire.
Our aime is at your smile if you but say
ffalts merit pardon when as children play.   [1900]
We haue our end and thinke it greater prays
Then if the muses nine shold bring vs bays.
No cretiks censure wee'l regard if you
Approue our play to whom tis only dew.

FINIS.   [1905]

[Fol. 38v]
1897 *sir,*] read *Sirs,*

NOTES

NOTES

Citations are made, without further reference, to authors and plays in the following editions:

Thomas Randolph: *The Drinking Academy*, ed. H. E. Rollins and S. A. Tannenbaum, Cambridge, Mass., 1930. All other references are to *The Poetical and Dramatic Works of Thomas Randolph*, ed. W. Carew Hazlitt, 2 vols., London, 1875.

Ben Jonson: *The Masque of Queens*, printed in *Masques and Entertainments*, ed. Henry Morley, The Carisbrooke Library, IX, London, 1890. All other references are to *Ben Jonson*, ed. C. H. Herford and Percy Simpson, 6 vols., Oxford, 1927-38.

James Shirley: *The Dramatic Works of James Shirley*, ed. Alexander Dyce, 6 vols., London, 1833.

THE SPEAKERS

Line

5 *Politico*] The name is perhaps drawn from Sir Politick Would-be in Jonson's *Volpone*. See note to l. 236. But see also "A Character, Aulico-politico-Academico," the title of a poem by Randolph (*Poems*, ed. Thorn-Drury, p. 134).

6 *Loserello the ffairy Knight*] Cf. *Amyntas*, dramatis personae (I, 271), "Jocastus, a fantastic shepherd and a fairy knight." Lazarillo is the hero of the novel *Lazarillo de Tormes*, and a character in *The Woman Hater* (1606) by Beaumont and Fletcher. The present name is perhaps a punning adaptation.

7 *Spendall*] In Randolph's *Hey for Honesty*, II. iv (II, 415), Penia-Poverty is called the "eldest daughter of Asotus-Spendall." Spendall's name comes from a prodigal in Jonson's *Eastward Hoe* (1604). The name is also found in J. Cooke's *Greenes Tu-Quoque* (1609-12).

8 *Couet*] Lady Covet is a character in Thomas May's *Old Couple* (1619-36).

9 *Craft a Cheater*] Cf. *The Drinking Academy*, Speakers, l. 9, "Timothy Sheirke a cheater."

10 *Snap*] A character in Fletcher's *Beggar's Bush* (1622).

Shift] A character in Jonson's *Every Man Out of his Humour* (1599) and also in William Percy's *Cuck Queans* (1601).

18 *Barresters*] Only one Barrister speaks in the play unless the Barrister of V. v is different from the one in V. vi. Probably the setting as a law court called for several mutes as Barristers.

NOTES

19 *Elues*] Probably acted by the same young children who were disguised as "ffaries" in the list of Craft's companions in the cheat. Elves were considered in some way subservient to fairies, and could be sent by the fairies to pinch mortals. See M. W. Latham, *The Elizabethan Fairies* (New York, 1930), pp. 20-21.

20 *Iudges &c:*] Mutes in V. v, vi.

The Prologue and Play

2-3 *Not in heigh numbers . . . scene*] Cf. the Prologue to *Amyntas* (I, 269):

> Gentlemen, look not from us rural swains
> For polished speech, high lines, or courtly strains.

Cf. also "To the Reader," *The Jealous Lovers* (I, 56), "I confess no heights here, no strong conceits; I speak the language of the people."

11 *Scæna 1ᵃ*] The place is a street. *1ᵃ* is the abbreviation for *prima*.

34 *condeme it*] Cf. *The Jealous Lovers*, III. iv (I, 114), "condemn a bag; let trash away"; *The Drinking Academy*, l. 144, "condemn 2 bags of a 1000 pounds a peace."

ppetual imprisment] See also ll. 37-8, 47-8, 920-1. The legal phrase for life imprisonment; a favorite although conventional image with Randolph: cf. *The Muses' Looking Glass*, II. iv (I, 213), "The chuff's crowns imprison'd in his rusty chest"; also *The Jealous Lovers*, I. i (I, 70) and *Hey for Honesty*, I. iii (II, 403). For Randolph's constant use of "perpetual," see *The Muses' Looking Glass*, III. ii (I, 224), *The Jealous Lovers*, I. iv, IV. vii (I, 77, 149), *Hey for Honesty*, I. iii, II. iv (II, 404, 416).

37 *Ile to court*] The first impulse of the prodigal Quicksilver in *Eastward Hoe*, II. ii. 57-8.

40 *apparitor*] An inferior officer who summoned delinquents to the spiritual court. Cf. *The Muses' Looking Glass*, I. i (I, 181), "Bailiffs, promoters, jailors, and apparitors."

42 *mouldy bagges and coffers*] Cf. also l. 921. Cf. *The Jealous Lovers*, III. vii (I, 126), "lie with your musty bags," *The Drinking Academy*, l. 790, "in to mouldy coffers me confin'd."

45-6 *send goulden angels to the diuil*] A common pun, here with the added play on the Devil Tavern where Spendall is to spend the money. Cf. *Hey for Honesty*, IV. i (II, 449).

51 *Scæna 2ᵃ*] The same.

53 *It begins to worke*] Perhaps we are to assume that Craft has sent Spendall to Covet in order to ensnare them both, and now he sees Covet's greed operating as he has planned.

NOTES

54-6 *I may chance . . . fashon*] An instance of the extra familiarity between actor and audience to be expected in a privately performed play. The boy is commenting on his make-up and costume which have prevented his recognition by the audience. Perhaps the reference to "Lady like" indicates a boy who had taken a female rôle in the previous Latin play of the festivities.

57-8 *an 88 Armado*] Cf. also *Aristippus* (I, 12) and *Hey for Honesty*, IV. iii (II, 469). Cf. Jonson's *Alchemist*, IV. iv. 29, and *The Magnetick Lady*, I. vi. 17-18:

> an invasion,
> Another eighty eight, threatning his Countrey.

60-3 *Hanse van Verking Snort . . . selues*] See the Introduction, pp. xxxi ff. The reference as applied to Dirck Bas is not crystal clear, owing to the variety of meanings and possible puns contained in the word "states," which is used, for example, in line 88 in a strained sense as "stationers." English commissioners had been sent to Holland in 1618-19 to negotiate with Bas but had failed. The general meaning of the reference, then, is probably to the fresh set of commissioners or "new states" whom Bas is now meeting in England. A complicated pun is also probably intended in a play on words of "states" as the United Provinces and perhaps also the Indies. To thread such a labyrinth, in which Randolph delighted, one might translate the pun: Bas has arrived to bribe the new states (English commissioners) so that the old states (the former set of commissioners who had failed, with the subsidiary meanings of the Indies, the United Provinces, and the states of England and the Provinces concerned in the old quarrel) may now be at peace, with past failures forgotten. Dr. Dirck Bas, Knight, and his commission were in England from December 5, 1621, to February 12, 1623.

65-6 *I beleue you guesse . . . allready*] So two other of Randolph's characters in private plays introduce themselves to the audience. Cf. *The Conceited Pedlar* (I, 38), "But I see you have a great desire to know what profession I am of"; and *The Drinking Academy*, ll. 256-7, "you may gues my profession I am on that. . . ."

68 *land fisher*] Cf. *The Jealous Lovers*, V. iv (I, 143), "Thou and I have been land-pirates."

70 *I thanke my stars*] See also ll. 94, 137. For the phrase, cf. *The Conceited Pedlar* (I, 38); *Hey for Honesty*, III. iii (II, 444, 445).

73 *Æsops cat*] The fable of the Cat and the Chicken. Cf. *Hey for Honesty*, II. i (II, 404), "What an Œsopical roaring lion am I."

76 *Scæna 3ᵃ*] The same. According to this classical system of scene division, found in all of Randolph's five-act plays, the scene technically changes

NOTES

with the entrance of any character although for dramatic purposes there is no break. Academic drama customarily employs this system.

86-7 *O tempora O moribus!*] Cf. the comic schoolmaster in Philip Sidney's *Lady of May* (*Works*, ed. Feuillerat, II, 331-2), "*O Tempori, ô Moribus!*"

88 *states*] I.e., estates, the stationers or writers.

93 *Scena 4ª*] The same.

97-8 *Africke Asia and 3 parts of America*] See also ll. 1027-8. Cf. *The Conceited Pedlar* (I, 37), "the Asia of the Dolphin, the Africa of the Rose, and the America of the Mitre"; *The Muses' Looking Glass*, III. iv (I, 234), "all Europe, Asia, and Africa too; but in America and the new-found world."

104 *I discouer . . . 7 stars*] So Dapper is assured in *The Alchemist*, I. ii. 123-24:

>   Well, a rare starre
> Raign'd, at your birth.

106-7 *when she kist him in his cradle*] Cf. *The Alchemist*, I. ii. 150, "Not, since she kist him, in the cradle."

114 *Cam*] I.e., the Great Cham.

121-2 *vaine in your forehead . . . palmistry*] Cf. Shirley's *Love in a Maze*, I. i (II, 279), "Look in my forehead, have you any skill in palmistry?"

123-4 *fame . . . fil her goulden trumpet only with yʳ name*] See also ll. 179-80. Cf. *The Muses' Looking Glass*, III. iv (I, 237-8):

> When Fame hath taken cold, and lost her voice,
> We must be our own trumpets. . . .
> Other men's mouths become your trumpeters
> And winged fame proclaims you loudly forth.

Cf. also *The Jealous Lovers*, III. iii (I, 115):

> Boreas shall blow my trumpet, till I spread
> Thy fame.

126-8 *I might haue vewed . . . tel me of*] Cf. *The Drinking Academy*, ll. 373-5, "deare bird lets in I am afier till I se a looking glase and vew all thes wounders thou speakest of"; *The Jealous Lovers*, III. vi (I, 123):

> That I should have so ravishing a face,
> And never know it! Miser that I was!
> I will go home and buy a looking glass
> To be acquainted with my parts hereafter.

NOTES

Hey for Honesty, I. ii (II, 398), "O heavens! can I do all these things you talk of?"

138-9 *12 giants an hower . . . fury*] Cf. Shirley's *Young Admiral*, III. i (III, 138), "I will kill my hundred men an hour for a twelvemonth."

147 *crumbs of comfort*] Probably an allusion to *Crumbs of Comfort* by Michael Sparke, entered in the Stationers' Register on October 7, 1623. The earliest edition known is dated 1628. For books similarly mentioned, see *Hey for Honesty*, III. iii (II, 443) and *The Muses' Looking Glass*, III. iv (I, 234).

148-9 *fary wich whos spel . . . no difficulty*] In Cartwright's *Ordinary*, II. ii (Hazlitt's Dodsley, XII, 233) the cheaters engaged in making a gull believe himself valiant ask, "Would you fight fair, or conquer by a spell?" to which the gull answers, "I do not care for witchcraft; I would have my strength rely merely upon itself."

153-4 *Was not s^r Amides . . . inchanted*] A conventional incident in romances. Cf. Shirley's *Love Tricks*, V. iii (I, 88), "have read in histories, and relations, kernicles, very famous knights, and prave sentilmen of valors, and shivalries, have been enchanted."

154-5 *did feats . . . heare of*] Cf. Shirley's *Young Admiral*, III. i (III, 128), "live to make nations stand a tiptoe to hear thy brave adventures."

156 *am I, I an s^r Huen*] I.e., am I. Ay, if Sir Huon.

158 *I shall loue wich craft as long as I liue*] Cf. Shirley's *Young Admiral*, III. i (III, 129), "I should love witches the better while I live"; *Hey for Honesty*, I. ii (II, 398), "I shall love a *Nosce teipsum* as long as I live."

159 *Scæna Quinta*] The same.

165 *Oberon*] Here conceived, for the purposes of the intermittent satire on Spain, as the king of England. Elizium, or fairyland, therefore represents England, as conventionally in Spenser's *Faerie Queene*, Copley's *Fig for Fortune*, and Dekker's *Whore of Babylon*. See especially l. 226 below.

172 For similar definiteness in time, see for example, *Hey for Honesty*, I. ii (II, 401); *The Drinking Academy*, ll. 568-9.

173 *exit Losserel*] Unless Craft is to call out ll. 174-5 after the departed, or departing, Losserello, it would seem the writer placed the stage-direction too early merely to take advantage of the empty space in the half line.

176 *It shall be so America is ours*] Read *so. America*. Politico is commenting upon the letter he has just finished reading, which we may suppose to have been written by Craft as the preliminary to the cheat.

178 *gemmes the red sea boast*] Cf. *The Muses' Looking Glass*, IV. i (I, 241):
                therefore wear the jewels
Of all the East; let the Red Sea be ransack'd
To make you glitter.

NOTES

183-4 *earth borne broud . . . shelter*] See also ll. 456-7, 1080-1. Cf. *The Jealous Lovers*, II. v, xii (I, 98, 108):

> bold as that earthborn race
> That bade Jove battle, and besieg'd the gods.
> . . . .
> Couldst thou retreat into thy mother's womb,
> There my revenge should find thee.

Cf. also Shirley's *Young Admiral*, I. ii (III, 105), "and make 'em creep into the earth again."

189 *pouerty I euer banish thee the earth*] Cf. *The Drinking Academy*, ll. 499-500, "a mine of gold in Worldlies house shall bind pleasure to vs and for euer banish pouerty our company."

192 *liquid golden*] Some error in the copying. Either a following noun has been omitted, or we should read *liquid gold* or *golden liquid*.

197 *ffrō fairy. [o doth]*] Probably the start of an augmentation concluding in l. 218 when Politico asks, "Doth not the mighty Oberon rule ther?"

198-9 *to in rich nature . . . besids*] Read *inrich*. A satirical reference to the prodigality of fashionable attire in England.

211-2 *bey with prouinces*] Cf. *The Young Admiral*, III. i (III, 134), "purchase smiles with provinces."

222 *beads*] I.e., beds.

228 *fiend out*] The writer probably began to write *that* after *fiend*, but after forming the initial *t* he decided to insert *out* between the two words. He thereupon formed the *o* over the *t* and wrote the *out*, afterward forgetting to add *that* before *happy*.

236-7 *name suets with his nature . . . Politico*] Cf. Jonson's *Volpone*, I. v. 102-3:

> Sir, this knight
> Had not his name for nothing, he is politique.

flamen] a title employed in *Amyntas* (I, 288, 357).

243-4 *Politico is found . . . king*] Note the similar break from prose into a couplet in *Hey for Honesty*, I. i (II, 388-9).

254-6 *bring 7. sufficient vserers . . . yeares*] Cf. *The Drinking Academy*, ll. 619-20, "Ile bring you 12 sufficient vserers all Iews of his one tribe, that shall sweare this is my legitimat father."

261 *Let thy returne be suddaine*] Cf. *The Drinking Academy*, ll. 520-1, "let your returne be suddane," *The Jealous Lovers*, III. v (I, 122), "Drink on, for our return shall sudden be."

267 *Actus secundus*] Supply *Scæna 1ª*. The place is the street outside Covet's house.

NOTES

271 *drife foot*] I.e., dry foot. A standard phrase applied to hunting with bloodhounds. Cf. *The Comedy of Errors* (*Works*, ed. Kittredge), IV. ii. 39; *Every Man in his Humour* (1616), II. iv. 9.

284-5 *vserers house it is so baracadoed*] Cf. *The Jealous Lovers*, IV. ii (I, 136):

> Have I not barricadoed all my doors,
> And stopp'd each chink and cranny in my house,
> To keep out poverty and lean misfortune?

286 *Ser: Sir who are you*] The entrance of this character should start *Scene* 2. The place remains the same.

297 *Scæna 3ᵃ*] The same.

302 *I dare not lie alone*] Cf. *Hey for Honesty*, IV. iii (II, 464), "How do you think I can endure to lie alone, when so many sprites are walking?" *The Muses' Looking Glass*, II. ii (I, 199):

> no more such terrible stories;
> I would not for a world lie alone to-night.

306 *my house is hanted*] Cf. *The Alchemist*, V. iv. 10-11:

> I haue beene faine to say, the house is haunted
> With spirits, to keepe churle back.

335 *Scena 4ᵃ*] The place alters, presumably to Craft's house.

338-9 *Imediatly Losserello . . . hower*] Cf. *The Young Admiral*, IV. i (III, 144), "he's mad to be enchanted"; *The Drinking Academy*, ll. 668-70, "Knowlittle will be vpon vs immediately. I had much ado to staue him of frō comeing along with me he is so affire to court maddam Pecunia."

340-3 *he can not . . . marquet is spoiled*] Cf. *The Alchemist*, III. v. 72-3:

> He must not see, nor speake
> To any body, till then.

344-5 *fech instantly the clothes . . . players*] In *The Alchemist*, IV. vii. 67-8, Drugger is advised by the rogues to borrow his Spanish disguise from the players.

345 *yester day*] An error. Craft had made an appointment with Losserello to be enchanted three hours after their first meeting in ll. 172-5. The time element in the play may perhaps have been telescoped from the original version (see ll. 510, 1307).

347-8 *Pentlow hill*] The town of Pentlow is on the northern border of Essex. There was a considerable witch scare in Essex in the late 1580's but so far as can be discovered Pentlow was not associated with the trials at St. Osyth's or the accused witches. There may be, of course, a personal

NOTES

reference applying to the actor, and the old witch trials in Essex could have been recalled in connection with the county of his birth. It seems farfetched to conjecture that *Pentlow* is a mistake for *Pendle* which was associated with the Lancashire witches in 1633. Witchcraft in Essex is referred to as late as 1616 in Jonson's *Devil Is An Ass*, I. ii. 24.

350 *make hast . . . else*] Cf. *The Drinking Academy*, l. 658, "Iack lets hast and dresse for feare we be to late."

351-2 *here hast let me . . . person*] Cf. *The Drinking Academy*, l. 660, "I pray yᵒ stay I haue more need of dressing then you."

355-6 *you are so peuish . . . clothes*] Cf. *The Drinking Academy*, l. 700, "You are so imperious, pray come you and helpe to."

363 *thou needest none, thy face is like a visard*] Cf. *The Drinking Academy*, ll. 661-2, "Your face wold scare any body. it is a pretty natural visard you haue on"; *The Muses' Looking Glass*, I. iii (I, 184):

> We want you to play Mephistopheles.
> A pretty natural vizard.

Cf. Beaumont and Fletcher, *A King and No King* (1611), "I marry am I afraid of my face. Thou wouldst be *Philip* if thou sawst it in a glass; it looks so like a Visour." (*Works*, ed. Waller, I, 176).

For vizards associated with fairies and witches, see Jonson's *Masque of Queens* (p. 103), "at their convents or meetings, where sometimes also they are vizarded and masked"; *The Merry Wives of Windsor* (*Works*, ed. Kittredge), IV. iv. 70.

385-6 *Orpheus like with a Iews harpe*] Cf. *The Jealous Lovers*, III. iv (I, 114):

> Is Clio dumb, or has Apollo's Jew's-trump
> By sad disaster lost her melodius tongue?

For Orpheus and a jew's-trump, see Shirley's *Opportunity*, IV. i (III, 426).

387 *some body . . . betraide*] Cf. *The Drinking Academy*, ll. 705-7, "here is Knowlittle and his tribe all ready. lets in or we are betray'd."

388 *Scæna 5ᵃ*] The same.

404-5 *ten in the hundred*] See the Introduction, p. 000.

406-7 *heaps of gould . . . brouding ouer*] Cf. *The Drinking Academy*, ll. 132-3, "go brode ouer your mouldy bags and hach more mony"; *The Muses' Looking Glass*, II. iv (I, 211), "No, sit and brood on thy estate: as yet it is not hatch'd into maturity"; *The Jealous Lovers*, I. i (I, 69):

> And when I brooding sit upon my bags,
> And euery day turn o'er my heaps of gold.

409 *Scæna 6ᵃ*] The same.

NOTES

413-5 *growene purblind . . . candle light*] Cf. *Hey for Honesty*, III. iii (II, 441), "Many treasurers, sequestrators, and receivers came for help, for they had received so much moneys, that they had lost their eyesight, and could not see to make accounts."

423 *brace of babones*] Cf. *The Drinking Academy*, l. 498.

424 *bring mony with him besids*] In *The Alchemist*, I. ii. 172-3, Dapper is bid to bring 20 nobles to distribute among the queen's servants. Cf. Politico selling his lands to give a largesse to Oberon's servants (ll. 264-5).

426-7 *gould finches boyes . . . take the birds*] Cf. *The Young Admiral*, IV. i (III, 145), "have you no goldfinches in your fob?" *The Drinking Academy*, l. 261, "I am a fouler and my game is gold finches or fine white siluer birds."

432 *You mungril . . . better words*] Cf. *The Drinking Academy*, l. 703, "Reason good y° mungril."

434 *peare of mastiue . . . snarling*] Cf. *The Jealous Lovers*, III. v (I, 121), "Brawling, you mastiffs?"

435-6 *I will make you both haks meat*] Cf. Peter Hausted's *Rival Friends* (1632), sig. M2^v:

> And when I'ue done, will *fillip* that *morsell*, woman,
> On an embassage to my Hawkes. . . .
> He sweares he will make *hawkesmeat* of my daughter.

See also J. C., *The Two Merry Milkmaids* (1620), sig. F3^v, "For this Tongue shall be pull'd out, and throwne vnto the Dogges, or to the Hawkes, before it shall offend."

439-40 *s'lid I heare . . . raskals*] Cf. *The Drinking Academy*, l. 705, "S'lid I heare musicke . . . lets in."

441 *Scæna 7^a*] The same.

443 *durty acres*] A phrase borrowed from Shirley: cf. *The Traitor*, IV, i; *Love's Cruelty*, III. i; *The Ball*, II. i (II, 158, 222; III, 20).

456-7 *Ile be y^r captaine . . . Olympus*] See also ll. 183-4. Cf. *The Muses' Looking Glass*, II. ii (I, 203):

> O, that the valiant giants would again
> Rebel against the gods, and besiege heaven,
> So I might be their leader.

461-2 *and let in day*] See note to ll. 700-2.

464 *Screach owle besilent*] Cf. *Amyntas*, III. iv (I, 326):

> Dar'st thou screech-owl,
> With thy rude croaking interrupt their music.

467 *thy breath is infectious*] Cf. *Hey for Honesty*, IV. i (II, 453), "Thy very breath's infectious."

NOTES

484-6 *shold he hide . . . light me to him*] Plagiarized from Beaumont and Fletcher, *A King and No King* (1611):

> Nay never hide yourself; or were you hid
> Where earth hides all her riches, near her Center;
> My wrongs without more day would light me to you.
>
> (*Works*, ed. Waller, I, 199)

486 *iust angre*] A favorite adjective with Randolph: see ll. 464, 489, 502, 511. For "just anger," cf. *The Jealous Lovers* (I, 97, 108) and *The Muses' Looking Glass* (I, 262). For "just" used with other nouns, cf. *The Jealous Lovers* (I, 77, 165).

490 *deare*] I.e., dare.

491-2 *Did furies guarde . . . kill him*] Cf. *The Young Admiral*, IV. v (III, 164):

> Did you else grasp an empire, and your person
> Guarded with thunder, I would reach and kill you.

Cf. also *Hey for Honesty*, I. i (II, 386), "though my hedge of teeth were a quickset, my tongue would through" and II. iv (II, 416), "her hunger will break through and devour us."

505 *I will make the vice Roy*] Cf. Jocastus to Mopsus in *Amyntas*, V. iv (I, 356), "For this I'll make thee augur to his grace." In Shirley's *Opportunity*, III. ii (III, 409), Pimponio, pretending to be a prince, promises Ascanio who is assisting in the mock-gulling:

> prove but a witch,
> I'll make thee one of my privy counsellors.

527 Supply *exeunt*.

529 *Scena 1ª*] The place remains in Craft's house.

547 *I shall creepe in to his company*] Cf. *Every Man in his Humour* (1616), I. iv. 67-8, "now dos he creepe, and wriggle into acquaintance with all the braue gallants."

573 *Scæna 2ª*] The same.

574-8 *Here she is . . . kisse the diuil*] Cf. *The Young Admiral*, IV. i (III, 144-5):

> *Did.* That is she.
> *Paz.* That old hag?
> *Did.* Good words; she has come two hundred mile today upon a distaff, salute her, she expects it.
> *Paz.* Would you have me kiss the devil?

579 *downe one your knees and [wri*]*] Probably the start of an augmentation which concludes in l. 582.

NOTES

582-3 *downe one y^r knees . . . presence*] Cf. *The Alchemist*, V. iv. 21-2:

> Downe o' your knees, and wriggle:
> Shee has a stately presence.

Cf. *Amyntas*, II. vi (I, 306), "Does not King Oberon bear a stately presence."

583-4 *most lerned maddam of the laplanders*] Cf. *The Young Admiral*, IV. i (III, 146), "Great lady of the Laplanders . . . your learned beldamship." Cf. *Hey for Honesty*, IV. ii (II, 459), "beldame of Lapland." The Lapland witches are frequently referred to in the drama: cf. Beaumont and Fletcher, *The Chances*, V. iii, and *The Fair Maid of the Inn*, IV. i (*Works*, ed. Waller, IV, 237; IX, 199).

584 *this gentleman my pretious friend*] Cf. *The Young Admiral*, IV. i (III, 145):

> This is the gentleman. . . .
> He is a precious friend of mine.

586 *implores y^r powerful spels*] Cf. *The Young Admiral*, IV. i (III, 145), "For whom I do beseech your powerful spells."

587-9 *if y^r beldameship . . . you haue*] Cf. *The Young Admiral*, IV. i (III, 145):

> Nor for this benefit, shall you find him only
> Obedient to yourself, but very dutiful
> To any devil you have.

590 *Thou woldst not . . . wich*] Cf. *The Young Admiral*, IV. i (III, 145), "Thou wouldst not have me lie with the old witch?"

592 *not capable of incantation*] Cf. *The Young Admiral*, IV. i (III, 144), "that he may be capable of the charm."

592-3 *any thing transitory about him*] Cf. *The Alchemist*, III. v. 30, "Keepe nothing, that is transitorie, about you."

603-4 *our spel . . . about him*] Cf. *The Young Admiral*, IV. i (III, 145), "no charms can fasten on you then, her spells can have no power, if you do not throw it away instantly."

608-9 *trubled to haue the diuil search him*] Cf. *The Alchemist*, III. v. 25-6:

> her *Grace* will send
> Her *Faeries* here to search you.

615 *In my fob*] Cf. *The Young Admiral*, IV. i (III, 145), "have you no goldfinches in your fob?"

NOTES

621 *Child*] Cf. *The Young Admiral*, IV. i (III, 145), "He is welcome, child."

call in Mistophiles] Cf. *The Young Admiral*, IV. i (III, 145), "Where is Mephistophiles?"

622 *Now are you in a fine picle*] Cf. *The Young Admiral*, II. ii (III, 121), "if I was not in a sweet pickle."

625-6 *not more then a crowne . . . M^{rs} gaue*] Cf. *The Alchemist*, III. v. 43-4:

> I ha' nothing but a half-crowne
> Of gold, about my wrist, that my loue gaue me.

627-8 *And wold y^o . . . 20 crownes away*] Cf. *The Alchemist*, III. v. 46-8:

> And, would you incurre
> Your aunts displeasure for these trifles? Come,
> I had rather you had throwne away twentie half-crownes.

630 *as y^o loue y^r selfe confesse*] Cf. *The Young Admiral*, IV. i (III, 145), "Away with it, as you love yourself."

632 *so pinch y^o your body*] In *The Alchemist*, III. v. 33-42. The fairies pinch Dapper until he disburses.

634-5 *if y^o haue . . . thanke y^r selfe*] Cf. *The Young Admiral*, IV. i (III, 146), "if you dissemble, and be kill'd afterward, thank yourself"; and IV. iii (III, 157), "I had like to have my brains beaten out."

636-7 *I haue not . . . mony*] Cf. *The Young Admiral*, IV. i (III, 146), "I defy him that has any thing in the likeness of coin."

641-2 *we may stroake him*] Cf. *The Alchemist*, V. iv. 29, "Let me now stroke that head."

642 *begin the Orgies*] See note to l. 799.

648 *Oh ho ho!*] Losserello bellows when the witch strokes his head.

655 *Cerberus his fome*] In one of the notes to his *Masque of Queens* (p. 118, n. 3), Jonson mentions "Cerberus's foam." The reference is to the foam from Cerberus's mouth which became aconite as he struggled against Hercules. See Ovid's *Metamorphoses*, VII, 406-19, 660, 788.

658-9 *Bring with y^o . . . sacred iuce*] Cf. *The Young Admiral*, IV. i (III, 146), "Have you brought that sacred juice."

659 *of Lethe's well*] Probably drawn from Horace, *Epode* V, 26, "spargens Avernalis aquas." Cf. also Tomkis's *Albumazar*, I. vii (Hazlitt's Dodsley, XI, 325):

> With these walk as unwounded as Achilles
> Dipp'd by his mother Thetis.

NOTES

660 *poison of Æchidne*] Probably Cerberus's foam (see note to l. 655). Cf. Ovid's *Metamorphoses*, VII, 408-9:

> illud Echidneae memorant e dentibus ortum
> esse canis

661 *Wee'l make him ... mad as we be*] Cf. Middleton's *Witch*, V. ii (Mermaid, II, 189), "Those will make the younker madder."

664-6 *I am not acquainted ... enchantment*] Cf. *The Young Admiral*, IV. i (III, 146), "he does not know the constitution of every devil, and to make too many acquainted, if he could be finished otherwise, your art may dispence."

673 *Ye nimble ffaunes and siluans all*] Cf. *The Witch*, I. ii (Mermaid, II, 130), "Hags, Satyrs, Pans, Fawns, Sylvans." Middleton's source was Scott, *Discoverie of Witchcraft*, "*hags*, fairies, *satyrs, pans, faunes, sylens.*"

675 *Gether hemlocke*] Cf. Jonson's *Masque of Queens* (p. 112):

> I have been plucking, plants among,
> Hemlock, henbane

677 *Gather night shade*] Cf. *The Masque of Queens* (p. 113), "Nightshade, moon-wort."

679 *molds eyes*] A pleasantry, since moles were popularly supposed to have no eyes. Cf. *The Muses' Looking Glass*, II. iii (I, 207), "How happy are the moles, that have no eyes!" For a similar pleasantry, see *adders eares*, l. 788. The eye of a bird or animal found a place in most charms: Cf. *The Masque of Queens* (p. 113), "I scratched out the eyes of the owl before"; *Macbeth* (*Works*, ed. Kittredge), IV. i. 14, "Eye of newt." The word *molds* has been so altered in the course of writing that the writer seems to have had something else in mind originally.

679 *adders tungs*] Cf. *The Masque of Queens* (p. 112), "Hemlock, henbane, adder's-tongue."

680 *crokeing toads lungs*] Cf. *The Masque of Queens* (p. 113), "I went to the toad breeds under the wall."

683 *poyson frõ the moone*] It was believed that when the moon was arrested in her course by the Thessalian witches and brought down to earth, it shed a kind of venomous foam upon certain plants, which were consequently much sought for. Cf. Lucan's *Pharsalia*, VI, 669, "et uirus large lunare ministrat"; also VI, 505-6:

> et patitur tantos cantu deprensa labores
> donec suppositas propior despumet in herbas.

686-8 *if it be to be eaten ... prepared my stomack*] In Middleton's *Witch*, I. ii (Mermaid, II, 134-5) Almachildes offers Hecate and Firestone various grisly delicacies for their meal. Hecate reciprocates by inviting him to sup with her, and Almachildes protests:

> How? sup with thee? dost think I'll eat fried rats
> And pickled spiders?

690-2 *Wher is my brasen knife . . . depest hell*] Cf. *The Masque of Queens* (p. 118):

> A rusty knife to wound mine arm;
> And as it drops I'll speak a charm
> Shall cleave the ground.

The writer perhaps substituted "brasen" for "rusty" on the authority of the description of Medea's knife in Ovid's *Metamorphoses*, VII, 227, "curvamine falcis aenae."

692 *faries*] The word in the manuscript is distinctly *faries*, and not *furies*. Some Elizabethans believe that hell was the abode of fairies. See M. W. Latham, *Our Elizabethan Fairies* (New York, 1930), pp. 109-10, 164 ff.

696 *spread thy sables*] Cf. *The Jealous Lovers*, V. iv (I, 161):

> Shall muffle up the lamentable world
> In sable clouds of grief and black confusion!

Cf. also *The Drinking Academy*, ll. 748-9:

> Wherfore the world hath now put on
> Thes sables to deplore

spangled skies] See also ll. 1004, 1077. Cf. *The Muses' Looking Glass*, IV. i (I, 241), "spangled the heavens with all those glorious lights."

697-702 *Hells power is contemned . . . aproching day*] Cf. *Aristippus* (I, 3-4):

> What! is my power contemn'd?
> Dost thou not hear my call, whose power extends
> To blast the bosom of our mother Earth?
> To remove heaven's whole frame from off her hinges,
> And to reverse all Nature's law?

Cf. also *The Masque of Queens* (p. 118):

> I beat you again, if you stay my thrice:
> Thorough these crannies where I peep,
> I'll let in the light to see your sleep!
> And all the secrets of your sway
> Shall lie as open to the day. . . .
> Shall cleave the ground, as low as lies
> Old shrunk-up Chaos.

NOTES

However, the delay in the Devil's arrival and his eventual appearance only under threat, seem to come directly from Lucan: cf. *Pharsalia*, VI, 742-4:

> tibi, pessime mundi
> arbiter, immittam ruptis Titana cauernis,
> et subito feriere die. paretis?

712 *Nor yet*] See the Introduction, p. ooo.

713-4 *Nay then Ile make . . . to night*] A paraphrase of the deleted lines which had imitated *The Masque of Queens* (p. 114):

> When we have set the elements at wars,
> Made midnight see the sun, and day the stars.

715-6 *shall make the mone . . . chariot come*] See the note to l. 683. Cf. *The Masque of Queens* (p. 114):

> When the pale moon, at the first voice down fell
> Poisoned, and durst not stay the second spell!

The writer, however, remembering that the moon itself was not poisoned but rather dispensed poison in its fall, tentatively interlined *efrighted* over *Poyson'd* and then forgot to make a final choice since neither is deleted. Cf. *The Jealous Lovers*, V. iv (I, 161), "methinks the sun Affrighted with our sorrows should run back."

718 *Nor yet my rage . . : obay my spell*] Cf. *The Masque of Queens* (pp. 117-8):

> Not yet! my rage begins to swell;
> Darkness, Devils, Night and Hell
> Do not thus delay my spell!

724-5 *what wil become . . . admiration the euent*] Cf. *The Young Admiral*, IV. i (III, 146):

> *Paz.* What must I do now?
> *Did.* Kneel down, and expect with obedience and admiration what will become on you.

737-8 *thou shalt be enchanted to*] So in *Amyntas*, V. vi (I, 365) Jocastus insists that his servant Bromius also join him in eating moly in order to share in the enchantment.

739 *Losserello del fumo*] This title may be a satirical jest on Losserello's "castles in the air," perhaps with a glance at alchemists. Cf. *Volpone*, II. ii. 156, "*blow, blow, puff, puff, and all flies* in fumo"; Beaumont and Fletcher, *The Mad Lover*, I. i (*Works*, ed. Waller, III, 9), "my small means are gone *in fumo*." Cf. *The Alchemist*, IV. v. 58.

NOTES

751 *Aconit ouergrone*] Cf. *The Masque of Queens* (p. 118):

> and Aconite
> To hurl upon this glaring light.

753-4 *Alecto's milke . . . vipers bloud*] Cf. *The Masque of Queens* (p. 116), "Both milk and blood." Cf. also Ovid, *Metamorphoses*, VII, 247, "alteraque invergens tepidi carchesia lactis."

757-8 *Here is sacred . . . wont to vse*] Cf. *The Young Admiral*, IV. i (III, 146):

> Have you brought that sacred juice
> Which at such a time we use?

759 *fine*] The writer seems to have started *fiend* before changing to *fine*.

771-2 *Cyprus bows . . . poppy*] Cf. *The Masque of Queens* (p. 113):

> Horned poppy, cypress boughs,
> The fig-tree wild.

774 *Killed a sextone*] Cf. *The Masque of Queens* (p. 111), "And frighted a sexton out of his wits."

779-81 *snaks bread . . . toads braine*] Cf. *The Masque of Queens* (p. 113):

> I went to the toad breeds under the wall,
> I charmed him out, and he came at my call.

782 *Well done my hag*] Cf. *The Masque of Queens* (p. 107), "Well done, my Hags!"

786 *meager hag*] Cf. Lucan, *Pharsalia*, VI, 515-6:

> tenet orae profanae
> foeda situ macies.

787-8 *I haue bin gathering . . . adders eares*] Cf. *The Masque of Queens* (p. 110):

> I have been gathering wolves' hairs,
> The mad dog's foam and the adder's ears.

789 *A mandrake . . . haue tore*] Cf. *The Masque of Queens* (p. 110):

> I last night lay all alone
> On the ground, to hear the mandrake groan;
> And plucked him up.

795 *This this*] Since the writer has a fondness for repetition, this example may not be a slip of the pen even though the metre is broken.

796 *childrens fat*] Cf. *The Masque of Queens* (p. 111), "Killed an infant to have his fat."

NOTES

797 *dead mens bones*] Cf. *The Masque of Queens* (p. 111):

> I have been choosing out this skull
> From charnel houses that were full.

798-9 *bassilisks bloud . . . Orgies you may begin*] In order to avoid the repetition of ll. 789-90, the deletion was made and this couplet borrowed from *The Masque of Queens* (p. 114):

> The basilisk's blood, and the viper's skin:
> And now our orgies let us begin.

Cf. also *Amyntas*, IV. viii (I, 344):

> What sad voice
> Disturbs our pious orgies?

801 *Whilst the maiecke timberils sound*] Cf. *The Masque of Queens* (p. 105), "and the timbrels play."

806 *Why ye raskall*] See also ll. 844, 1286, 1489. So Asotus in *The Jealous Lovers* (I, 113) calls his hangers-on "rascals," as does Dorylas in *Amyntas* (I, 329).

808 *So so my hags*] Cf. *The Witch*, V. ii (Mermaid, II, 189), "So, so, enough: into the vessel with it. There, 't hath the true perfection."

810-1 *Rise then . . . in the ground*] Cf. *The Masque of Queens* (p. 115):

> Come, let a murmuring charm resound
> The whilst we bury all i' the ground!

820-1 *the boyes will adore me . . . enchanted*] Cf. *The Young Admiral*, IV. iv (III, 159), "When I come home again, the poor fellows will fall down and worship me."

822-3 *an anticke Dance of wiches*] In *The Masque of Queens* (pp. 119-20) the witches dance "a magical dance, full of preposterous change and gesticulation." The writing of this direction necessitated the addition of ll. 761-7 vertically in the right hand margin of the page in order to provide the music; a piece of evidence helping to confirm a private performance.

824-5 *now each dispence . . . influence*] Cf. *The Young Admiral*, IV. i (III, 147):

> Thus on his shoulders I dispense
> My wand, to keep all bullets thence.

826 *Rub him . . . feele*] Cf. *The Young Admiral*, IV. i (III, 147), "Now rub his temples, forehead eke."

828 *Take him . . . pul it*] Cf. *The Young Admiral*, IV. i (III, 147):

> Give his nose a gentle tweak. . . .
> Take him by the hair, and pull it.

NOTES

829 *Oh, oh, O!*] A conventional outcry, but a favorite with Randolph: cf. *The Drinking Academy*, l. 797, "the diuil is come O o o!" and l. 822, "As I liue an other diuil O o o!" Cf. also *The Jealous Lovers* (I, 144, 145, 146) and *The Muses' Looking Glass* (I, 197, 256).

830 *He is now fre . . . bullet*] Cf. *The Young Admiral*, IV. i (III, 147), "Now his head's free from sword and bullet."

831 *Our charme is done*] Cf. *The Young Admiral*, IV. i (III, 147), "And now my potent charms are done."

832 *jam*] Probably a misreading of *ūam* [i.e., *unam*]. Hecate had not completely left the stage (see l. 847).

833 *am I sufficiently enchanted thinks thou*] Cf. *The Young Admiral*, V. iii (III, 178), "thou art sure I am sufficiently enchanted?" also IV. i (III, 148), "art thou sure I am enchanted now?"

834 *Thou art my Roseclero*] Cf. *The Young Admiral*, III. i (III, 128), "Thy whole body, triumphant, my Rosicleer"; also *The Drinking Academy*, ll. 496, 642.

thanke my grannam for it] Cf. *The Alchemist*, V. iv. 32, "Why doe you not thanke her *Grace*?"

840 *you haue fary-land enoufe*] Cf. *Amyntas*, V. vi (I, 365, 366), "We have enough beside in fairyland," and "You have enough beside in fairyland!" Cf. note to ll. 1629-35.

861 *Kisse her departing part*] Cf. *The Alchemist*, V. iv. 57, "Kisse her departing part."

862-3 *Is she gon . . . miles by this*] Cf. *The Young Admiral*, IV. i (III, 148):

> *Paz.* Whither is she gone now?
> *Did.* Home to a witch's upsitting; she's there by this time.
> *Paz.* Where?
> *Did.* In Lapland; she will cross the sea in an egg-shell, and upon land hath a thousand ways to convey herself in a minute.

871 *Scæna prima*] The place is a street, probably before Craft's house.

894 *giue fire*] For military terms applied to drinking, cf. *Aristippus* (I, 16-7). See also Shirley (II, 225; III, 406; VI, 298, 311).

895 *valiant sones of Mars*] See also l. 926. Cf. *The Jealous Lovers*, III. iv (I, 115), "Go, sons of Mars."

898 ff. The address of Spendall to his troops is very similar to the address of Penia-Poverty to her soldiers in *Hey for Honesty*, III. i (II, 428ff.), as is the rout of his men to the dispersing of Penia-Poverty's in III. ii.

902-3 *dared to call Mars cowerd*] Cf. *Hey for Honesty*, II. ii (II, 409), "Why Mars himself was an arrant coward to me."

NOTES

904 *your passiue fortitude*] Cf. *The Jealous Lovers*, II. viii (I, 104), "Twas but to exercise your passive valour."

906 *valiant hinder parts*] Cf. *The Jealous Lovers*, II. vi (I, 100):

> If your valour
> Lie in your back-parts, I will make experience
> Whether a kick will raise it.

So in *Hey for Honesty*, I. i (II, 387), Carion, threatened with a beating, retorts, "Why, and if it do, sir, you shall find that I have as valiant shoulders as another man."

919 *rat of Nilus*] Cf. George Sandys, *A Relation of a Journey* (ed. 1621), p. 101: "As for the Icnumon he hath but onely changed his name; now called the Rat of Nilus. A beast particular to Aegypt, about the bignesse of a Cat." The phrase was here apparently taken from Shirley, since it occurs in an outright borrowing from *The Traitor* in l. 1646. See also Shirley's *Love Tricks*, II. ii (I, 25).

919-20 *this monster . . . sacrelegious diuil*] Cf. *The Jealous Lovers*, IV. iv (I, 144), "This man—said I a man?—this monster, rather—but monster is too easy a name—this devil, this incarnate devil."

928 *Scæna 2ª*] The same.

965 *Scæna 3ª*] The same. But the place has become forgotten, since this scene apparently takes place indoors.

968 *How liks thou me now*] See also l. 383. So Dorylas, masquerading as Oberon in *Amyntas*, III. iv (I, 325), "How like you now my grace?"

981 *Scæna 4ª*] The same. There has been no break in the action between Scenes 1-2 and 3-4, yet the action in the last two scenes is better adapted to the interior of Craft's house than to the street. In l. 979 Shift asks whether it is "time to come in?"

982 *Eutacusticon*] The fairy diadem of l. 1001; actually an instrument to improve the sense of hearing. For mention of such an otacousticon, see *The Conceited Pedlar* (I, 46); also cf. Tomkis's *Albumazar*, I. iii (Hazlitt's Dodsley, XI, 315):

> Autocousticon!
> Why, 'tis a pair of ass's ears, and large ones.

986-7 *yʳ valior whch . . . wiser then Apollo*] A paraphrase of the deletion in ll. 493-4.

992-9 *Trew Presbiter Ihon . . . expatiat in*] Cf. *The Muses' Looking Glass*, III. ii (I, 223) for Chaunus and his boasts that various foreign countries have wooed him to be ruler.

NOTES

1006 *lin'd with fortunes apron*] In *The Alchemist*, III. v. 6-14, Dapper is invested in a robe made from the petticoat of Fortune, and blindfolded with a piece of her smock.

1011-12 *parg'd frō the dregs of mortality*] Cf. *Amyntas*, III. iv (I, 327):

>The fellow is a fool, and not yet purged
>From his mortality.

Cf. also *The Jealous Lovers*, IV. ix (I, 154):

>Receive me, new-created of a clay
>Purg'd from all dregs; my thoughts do all run clear.

Cf. also *Aristippus* (I, 17), "being purged and freed from so much earth."

1013 *flaimes more killing . . . thunder*] Cf. *The Drinking Academy*, ll. 74-5, "my eyes darts flames more killing then Ioues thunder."

1028-9 *it it*] An error caused by turning the page.

1040-1 *ffor a glorious sunne . . . horison*] Cf. *The Drinking Academy*, ll. 764-6:

>And let the sunnes your eyes
>Display ther goulden beames vpon
>This our obscured Horison.

1054-5 *safire is his skinne . . . richest Ruby*] Cf. *Amyntas*, V. vi (I, 364), "Thy sapphire ears and ruby nose." The image of a ruby nose from excessive drinking was a commonplace, but one of which Randolph was especially fond. See especially *Aristippus* (I, 11, 17); *The Conceited Pedlar* (I, 43); and *Hey for Honesty* (II, 422, 447).

1089 *Plum'd victory*] Cf. *The Jealous Lovers*, III. x (I, 130), "May plum'd victory wait on your sword."

1096 *Enter Losserello*] Scene 6 should properly begin with this entrance. The place is a street before Covet's house.

1100 *none yet apeare*] Cf. *The Jealous Lovers*, V. viii (I, 168), "No champion yet appear? I would fain fight."

1103-4 *open springs . . . crimson deluge*] See also ll. 1408-10. Cf. *The Drinking Academy*, ll. 78-9, "not all the blood wch flowes within thy veines tho it were an ocean able to make the world deluge"; ll. 167, 498-9, "spring a mine of gold." Cf. *Aristippus* (I, 11), "like a mad hogshead of March-beer that had run out, and threatened a deluge." Cf. *The Jealous Lovers*, III. iii (I, 112):

>But (like a torrent) overthrows the bank,
>As it would threat a deluge.

NOTES

Also cf. III. v (I, 117):

>   I will dispeople earth, and drown the world
>   In crimson floods and purple deluges.

Cf. also III. viii (I, 127), "I'll pledge thee though 'twere a deluge"; IV. vii (I, 148), "Break like a deluge of consuming fire."

1119 *Enter Spendall*] Scene 7 should properly begin with this entrance. There is no break in the action, and the place remains the same.

1120 *valiants*] *I.e.*, most valiant.

1135 *pyramids of Corinthian brasse*] See also ll. 184-5. Cf. *The Muses' Looking Glass*, III. i (I, 218), "Since Parian marble and Corinthian brass"; also III. i (I, 215-6) for pyramids as triumphal monuments.

1145 *scrach vp thy nymble perecranium*] Cf. *Hey for Honesty*, V. i (II, 475), "Nay, now I see thou hast some wit in thy pericranium."

1155 ff. With this farcical situation, cf. *The Jealous Lovers*, IV. iv (I, 144), "Now you have well spoke, why do you not, after all this rhetoric, put your hand behind you to receive some more instructions backward?"

1161 *lease of 9 to cats*] For jests on the lives of cats, see *Every Man in his Humour* (1616), III. i. 133-4; *Hey for Honesty*, II. iv (II, 417).

1218 *Scæna 7ª*] An error for Scene 8. The faulty numbering of scenes in this act is finally corrected at Scene 9, l. 1226. The place is probably the same.

1225 *present you immediatly*] *I.e.*, present Shift to Politico as a fairy attendant. See also ll. 1253, 1381.

1226 *Scæna 9*] The same.

1227 *earth bend vnder me*] Cf. *The Drinking Academy*, ll. 140-1, "the very ground bends to hould them."

1249-51 *O that he had . . . killing him*] Cf. Peter Hausted's *Rival Friends* (1632), sig. K3:

>   O that thou hadst
>   As many liues as haires that I might be
>   An age in killing thee.

See also Beaumont and Fletcher, *A King and No King* (1611):

>   but if all
>   My hairs were lives, I would not be engaged
>   In such a case to save my last life.
>   (*Works*, ed. Waller, I, 193)

1251-2 *tyme runnes on leaden wheles*] From the appearance of the word *wheles* under a strong glass it is just barely possible that the *w* was added later. For the image of time and leaden heels, see *Lingua*, III. iv (Hazlitt's Dodsley, IX, 391).

NOTES

1256 *an age in killing him*] Cf. Hausted's *Rival Friends* (1632), sig. K3:

> that I might be
> An age in killing thee.

1263 *Scæna 10*] The place is probably another street, near Craft's house.
1286-7 *thou visits Pluto*] Cf. *The Jealous Lovers*, V. viii (I, 168):

> He who dares pretend
> A title to a hair shall sup with Pluto.

Cf. *The Drinking Academy*, ll. 71-2, "send thee of an imbasage to Pluto."
1289 *Scæna 11*] The same.
1301 *I shall grow rusty . . . vse*] Cf. *The Young Admiral*, III. i (III, 130), "We shall be rusty here, for want of use."
1301-3 *I haue bin like to mutany . . . fight with all*] Cf. *The Young Admiral*, III. i (III, 130), "I shall go near to mutiny, and kill two or three of our own captains."
1314 *Well Ile go fech it? wilt thou go with me?*] The transcriber accidentally omitted this line which is essential to the sense of the next, and then squeezed in *Well Ile go fech it* with a pen like that of the text. The question mark after *it* and the still more necessary following words *wilt thou go with me?* are written with a much broader pen. It seems either the writer added these when he later discovered his first correction still did not properly introduce the next line, or else he changed pens in the middle of writing the whole line.
1317 *Snap art [thou] wher art thou?*] The writer obviously started to write *Snap art thou ther?* but changed his mind and forgot to delete the first *art* as well as *thou*.
1318 *I discouer light*] Cf. *The Drinking Academy*, ll. 769-71:

> S'lid I discouer.
> What Simple what?
> The day I thinke you call for here is a light comeing.

1319 *Scæna 12*] The same.
1326 Cf. *Hey for Honesty*, introduction (II, 382-3):

> Else, had I Morpheus' wand to charm your sight
> I'd close your eyes with slumber.

Cf. also *The Young Admiral*, IV. i (III, 147):

> Thus on his shoulders I dispense
> My wand.

1333 *Take this and this*] Cf. *The Jealous Lovers*, I. i (I, 69), "Take this, and this, and this, and this again."

NOTES

1344 *Scæna prima*] The street before Covet's house. Some sort of a balcony seems to be employed in this scene (see ll. 1382-3) although in default Politico and Shift could easily put their heads through an opening in the curtained rear of the stage.

1362 *I shall demolish . . . children*] Cf. *The Young Admiral*, III. i (III, 134), "Oh how I could demolish man, woman, and child now."

1370-1 *I am horriblely afraid . . . tremble*] Cf. *The Young Admiral*, IV. iv (III, 160), "now I begin, for all this, to be afraid; flesh will be flesh, and tremble."

1372-4 *this giant may be enchanted . . . on an other*] Cf. *The Young Admiral*, V. iii (III, 178), "my granam has given thee a spell too, so that we might fight our hearts out, afore we kill one another."

1374-6 *he may take me prisoner . . . gallace*] Cf. *The Young Admiral*, IV. iv (III, 160), "I may be taken prisoner by the enemy, and be hang'd afterward . . . what a dull rogue was I not to except the gallows in my conditions."

1390 *terræ filius*] A son of earth; *i.e.*, a man of obscure or illegitimate parentage, an upstart. Used as a general term of abuse. Also, an orator, formerly at the University of Oxford, privileged to make humorous and satirical strictures in a speech at the public "act."

1391 *this this*] Perhaps a slip of the pen, although such repetitions are common in Randolph.

1404 *Scæna 2°*] The same.

1408 *my eyes dart lightning*] Cf. *The Muses' Looking Glass*, III. iii (I, 230), "fury darts a lightning from your eyes."

1410 *deluge of deaths*] See the note to l. 1104.

1414 *shall*] From the formation of the letters it appears the writer may have intended *shalt* but forgot to cross the *t*. But for *thou shall*, see ll. 179, 1864.

1419 *tho it be but for my hanches*] Cf. *The Young Admiral*, III. i (III, 128), "cut into honourable collops, or have my haunches sod by a sutler's wife, and pass for camp mutton!" For another reference, see *The Jealous Lovers*, V. ii (I, 156), "I soldier's feed shall mince him."

1421 *cut thee in to collops*] See the quotation from *The Young Admiral*, note to l. 1419.

1423-4 *whipp'd with vipers by Tisiphone*] Cf. *The Jealous Lovers*, IV. v (I, 146):

> The worst is call'd Tisiphone
> Shall lash thee to eternity.

NOTES

1431-2 *Phœbus mounted . . . oer looke it*] See also ll. 1025-7. Cf. *The Muses' Looking Glass*, V. iii (I, 264):

> great Apollo
> Who . . . .
> Set in his car of light, surveys the earth
> From east to west.

1443 *O for euer Phœbus . . . bosome*] This could perhaps be a burlesque of the introduction to Hausted's *Rival Friends* which shows Sol reclining on Thetis's bosom.

1461 ff. With Politico's hanging-ballad compare Pantler making a comic ceremony of a hanging-ballad as he is led off to execution in Fletcher's *Bloody Brother*, III. ii. See also the farewell ballad of Quicksilver as he is led to prison in *Eastward Hoe*, V. v. 113 ff.

1491 *enter Snape*] Scene 3 properly begins with this entrance. The action is continuous and the place remains the same.

1507 *Scæna 3ᵃ*] Properly Scene 4. The place remains the same.

1541 *tho I had one foote in [the graue]*] Cf. *Hey for Honesty*, III. iii (II, 446), "With that one leg which was not yet i' th' grave."

1549 *Scæna 4ᵃ*] Properly Scene 5. The place is probably within Craft's house.

1556 *lord of the Antipodes and great Eutopia*] See also l. 1636, "earle of Eutopeia." Cf. *Amyntas*, I. iii (I, 279):

> out-talk the bravest parrot
> In Oberon's Utopia.

1560 *plumbeus intelects*] Cf. Sidney's *Lady of May* (*Works*, ed. Feuillerat, II, 335), "plumbeous cerebrosities."

1561 *My stately king of pigmies*] Cf. *Amyntas*, III. iv (I, 325):

> Walk not I
> Like the young Prince of Pigmies?

1565 *Scæna 5*] Properly Scene 6. The place remains the same.

1573-4 *a backe big enuf . . . fary honers*] Cf. *The Muses' Looking Glass*, II. i (I, 195):

> could your cruelty find
> No back but mine, you thought broad enough
> To bear the load of all these epithets?

1610-1 *thy heirrs be siluer*] See also l. 1651. "Silver hairs" was a favorite phrase with Randolph: cf. *The Jealous Lovers* (I, 112, 123, 125), *Hey for Honesty* (II, 404).

NOTES

1617-8 *knight of the cornu copia*] Cf. *Amyntas*, V. iv (I, 356):

> I am knight
> Of the mellisonant tingle-tangle.

Cf. also *Hey for Honesty*, V. i (II, 481), "dub me knight of the forked order." Jests on the cornucopia as the horn of plenty and the cuckold's horn are found in *Hey for Honesty*, II. v and III. iii (II, 424, 445); see also *Every Man in his Humour* (1616), III. vi. 23-5, and *Lingua*, III. vi (Hazlitt's Dodsley, IX, 405). Cf. *The Alchemist*, IV. vii. 41, "Or a Knight o' the *curious cox-combe*."

1626 *as I am a knight of the hornes*] So in *Amyntas*, V. vi (I, 363) Jocastus swears:

> by my knighthood,
> And by this sweet mellisonant tingle-tangle
> The ensign of my glory.

1627 *Of the cornu copia say*] So in *Amyntas*, V. iv (I, 356) Jocastus prefers the euphemism:

> I'll have't no more a sheep-bell; I am knight
> Of the mellisonant tingle-tangle.

1629-35 *I haue . . . a little durty earth . . . his dam the wich*] Cf. *The Alchemist*, V. iv. 59-60:

> SVB. But you must sell your fortie marke a yeare, now:
> DAP. I, sir, I meane. SVB. Or, gi't away: pox on't.
> DAP. I'le gi't mine aunt. Ile goe and fetch the writings.

1643 ff. The trial of Politico is largely drawn from Shirley's *Traitor*, but note the close resemblance to the sexton's mock trial of himself in *The Jealous Lovers*, IV. iv (I, 144), which may give some hints of the original scene here.

1643-5 *hold vp thy hand. . . . Not guilty*] Cf. *The Traitor*, III. i (II, 130), "First, Signior Depazzi, thou art indicted of high treason, hold vp thy hand; guilty, or not guilty? . . . Not guilty."

1646 *a traitor a villan a rat of Nilus*] Cf. *The Traitor*, III. i (II, 131), "yet like a wretch, a villain, a viper, a rat of Nilus."

1648-9 *ticle him vp . . . spiteful*] Cf. *The Traitor*, III. i (II, 130), "Rogero, tickle me, as thou lov'st thy lord; I do defy thee, spare me not, and the devil take thee if thou be'st not malicious."

1650-3 *Most illustrious . . . eer saw*] Cf. *The Traitor*, III. i (II, 131), "Most wise, most honourable, and most incorrupt judges, sleep not, I beseech you; my place hath called me to plead, in the behalf of my prince

NOTES

and country, against this notable, this pernicious, and impudent traitor, who hath plotted and contriued such high, heinous, and horrible treasons, as no age nor history hath ever mentioned the like."

1653-4 *this this is he . . . sufficient*] Cf. *The Traitor*, III. i (II, 131), "this fellow, not content to have his branches spread within the city."

1661 *attempt the sacr'd person of our prince*] Cf. *The Traitor*, III. i (II, 131), "he hath practised treasons against the sacred person of the duke."

1662-5 *treason vnderminding . . . blessed region*] A reference to the Gunpowder Plot. This allusion crops up in almost every play by Randolph: cf. *Aristippus* (I, 10); *The Conceited Pedlar* (I, 38); *The Muses' Looking Glass*, II. ii (I, 201); *Hey for Honesty*, I. ii, and II. iv (II, 401, 415). Philip of Spain is satirized in *Hey for Honesty* (II, 397, 448, 468).

1667-8 *Peace traitor . . . impudent*] Cf. *The Traitor*, III. i (II, 131), "Peace, sirrah, peace!—Nay, your lordships shall find him very audacious."

1668-70 *but seing this serpentine . . . attempt*] See also l. 437. Cf. *The Traitor*, III. i (II, 132), "and finding this serpentine treason broken in the shell,—do but lend your reverend ears to his next designs."

1677 *This this my lords condemnes him*] Cf. *The Traitor*, III. i (II, 133), "That, that, my lords, hath overthrown him."

1678-82 *this alone makes him guilty . . . guilty of treason*] Cf. *The Traitor*, III. i (II, 133), "I defy all the world that will hear a traitor speak for himself; 'tis against the law, which provides that no man shall defend treason, and he that speaks for himself, being a traitor, doth defend his treason."

1682-4 *and deserues . . . inuented*] Cf. *The Traitor*, III. i (II, 133), "for which he deserveth not only to die, but also to suffer tortures, whips, racks, strapadoes, wheels, and all the fiery brazen bulls that can be invented."

1690 *too*] I.e., two.

1697 *Scæna Sexta*] Properly Scene 7. The place remains the same.

1759 *senior*] I.e., señor.

1780 *Call in the elues . . . til he confes*] Cf. *The Alchemist*, III. v. 31-6:

> Looke, the *Elues* are come
> To pinch you, if you tell not truth. . . .
> They must pinch him, or he will neuer confesse, they say.

1781 *Ti ti ta ti*] Cf. the elves in *The Alchemist*, III. v. 34, "Ti, ti, ti, ti"; also III. v. 41, "Ti ti ti ti to ta." Cf. the fairies in *Amyntas*, III. iv. (I, 328), "ti ti ta ti."

1801-6 Another mock proclamation is found in *Hey for Honesty*, I. ii (II, 393).

NOTES

1817 *Is ther life . . . sacke*] So in *Amyntas*, II. vi (I, 308) the foolish Mopsus on being promised a place in fairyland, asks whether his own particular love is there: "But be there any Ladybirds there?"

1826 *Oberon not stored*] Some words such as *I am* seem to have been omitted between *Oberon* and *not*.

1847-8 *the first . . . of my famely*] Cf. *The Jealous Lovers*, I. i (I, 69):

> As I am a gentleman,
> And the first of all our family.

1858-9 *lord of all our Canary Ilands*] Cf. *Aristippus* (I, 33), "thou Catholic Monarch of Wines, Archduke of Canary."

1867-72 *Come set thee then vpon my throne . . . ha ha ha!*] Cf. *Amyntas*, V. vi (I, 366):

> In chairs of pearl thou plac'd shalt be,
> And empresses shall envy thee,
> When they behold upon our throne
> Jocasta with her ———— Dorylas.
> Ha, ha, ha!

1883 *Am I thus guld cheatd*] Cf. *Amyntas*, V. vi (I, 366), "Am I deceiv'd and cheated, gull'd and fool'd?"

1891 *let me die that my ghost . . . euerlastingly*] Cf. *The Jealous Lovers*, II. xiii (I, 109):

> But were my thread of life measur'd by his,
> I'd cut it off, though we both fell together;
> That my incensed soul might follow his,
> And to eternity prosecute my revenge.

www.ingramcontent.com/pod-product-compliance
Lightning Source LLC
Chambersburg PA
CBHW081831300426
44116CB00014B/2545